THE AUDIENCE ATTRACTION METHOD

The Smart Guide to Audience Building

Dawn Beth Baxter

BTD Studios

CONTENTS

The information given in this book should not
be treated as substitute for professional medical
advice; always consult a medical practitioner.

Any use of information in this book is at
the reader's discretion and risk.

Neither the author nor the publisher can be held
responsible for any loss, claim or damage arising
out of the use, or misuse, of the suggestions
made, the failure to take medical advice or for
any material on third-party websites.

DEDICATION

This Book belongs in the hearts of women who unapologetically want more for their lives than their standard lot. The fierce, the brave and the slaving away at their kitchen tables. **Pretties**, I dedicate it to the quiet moments of relief when your sales increase your earnings to a point where you don't have to worry about the bills this month. I dedicate it to the times you must choose between being a partner, friend, wife, mother, and CEO - often multiple times a day.

I dedicate this book to your dedication, to the pursuit of your dreams.

My purpose is tied in with you and it means everything to be able to live in a state that fulfils my personal purpose. You think me generous, but it has a selfish side.

This book however could not have come to be without some pretty epic souls.

As this is my first (and potentially my last) author offering I will be using this somewhat like an Oscars speech so strap in!

Dad, you instilled in me from a young age that I had a specialness about me that couldn't be replicated. 21 years of your love was enough to carry me through all of my days, however many I shall be blessed with. It is your belief in me that I stand upon still somewhere in the depths of my heart. You taught me more about gratitude in your passing than I could have ever realised at the time. You're proud. I just know it.

Mum, Despite not understanding what the hell I am going on about most of the time you smile, nod, listen and most importantly say yes to having my children so that I can pour myself into my life's work and legacy. You hold me up, often without a grumble in a simple, stable, and consistent warmth that sustains me. Thank you - I love you! I would stop reading now - you will likely be bored to death of the following contents, ha!

My sisters and brothers in law. Gillian and Su, we must think we are the Bronte sisters and I am not even sorry! Who do we think we are authoring books and sharing ideas with the entire world? I adore you and am so proud of you both. Turns out we really are entirely similar and nothing at all alike.

Bailey & Jack, Mum's been busy on and off for a while. I know especially during the rushed school run, the holidays when mum's half working and always whatsapping the studio you have found a way to understand how important this all is to me. You are proud, you are excited for me and you can see that dreams can come true and that means so much to me. I adore you both with every fibre of my being and you will always be my greatest joy and my most important offering to the world. I will love you forever, unconditionally, without reason, cause, or sense. Now get to bed!

To my team, all of you - I wouldn't be able to provide our pretties with the support and care I do without you now. You are the veins with which the blood rushes through. The electrical wire that carries the spark further. You keep me sane, caffeinated and surrounded by honest opinions and loving support. Who knew paying people to be your everyday work friends was such a wonderful thing? Stephanie, Emily, Kath, Su, Eilidh, Nikki, Nat, Lilly, Jade, Tasha, Lucy, Charlie, Thank you! You have contributed to something so much bigger than us. It's beautiful. I will be forever grateful for you and especially the HQ accent competitions and all the laughs!

Pretties - every moment you have given me, every penny spent, every sweet comment and belief has led me here on the wings you created for me. I adore you and will work tirelessly to continue to be the mentor/leader/friend you deserve.

Iain, As I write this on your bed, with your rock music playing in the background, adorned in your new Levi hoodie that is far too big for me, I remember how I fell in love with you at 14 years old.

Since that day you have taught me about life and love and myself more than any other human on the planet. The kind-hearted poet in you awakened something in me that once begun cannot be undone. Our life has been anything but a straight line. Thank you for the times of deep belief and pride. Thanks for paying for courses for me before we had the money, for encouraging me to leave employment to fly in my own direction despite the risk.

For bringing me coffee during all-nighters and helping with set plans and set-ups. I am grateful for the hard times, and the good times, for all of it has shaped me into the woman I am today. I like her a lot more than any of the previous versions. You love her still, despite her not being the woman you married. You could say you are the waves that have helped shape the stone of who I am standing before you today. You could say I owe it all to you. I will love you until the end of time and into the next dimension. There will always be a home for you in my heart, no matter what.

Anyway, wipe your eyes mateys, ahem, and let's get on with it shall we :)

INTRODUCTION

When we think of starting businesses, we often consider what we are good enough to make, sell or offer. We fear and want sales in equal measure, often considering that the influx of customers may become too much, our bank accounts overflowing with sales that dropped in from the heavens.

Throughout my entire career, the retail one, the corporate one, the creative one and now this CEO one, there has been one myth that has been busted repeatedly in multiple different ways.

"If you build it, they will come." Bullshit!

Sorry, Part of me being able to be of massive value to you is by being honest about what it is really like up here, in this multi 6 figure room that you may have made into something in your mind. I don't want to upset you but what you are imagining is probably entirely wrong.

Even now, every single connection I gain is on the back of consistent, focused, structured strategic work. I am not where I am by chance. My multi-millionaire clients are not where they are by chance.

You grow it, slowly and sometimes painfully over a period of time and then you maintain it.

Building an audience is a bit like spinning plates that have houseplants on them. Keep them spinning, keep them moving, keep the bloody plant ALIVE!

You may know you need an audience. You may even have an idea of what your dreamy clients look like. You may understand how to use Instagram, reels and even do a Facebook live. Sadly, these are subtexts to the main subject matter.

I am going to tell some brutal truths in this book, all will help you, despite feeling like a kick up the tush. I am going to give you the insider knowledge that master marketers who are neck deep in online sales daily have the honour of understanding.

Our privileged position in supporting so many clients in so many sectors allows us the chance to give you information you wouldn't be able to obtain without it.

Throughout these chapters, I am going to enlighten you as to how you can make audience-building part of the bedrock of your business and active business practices. I will show you the insider knowledge shared, passed, tried, and tested between millennial marketers that all but burned the degrees they obtained only to watch the industry shift again and again and again.

Inside these pages, we are going to walk a journey of the self, of messaging that goes beyond advertising your offers. We will look at psychology, design, consumer timing, social impact, genuine connection, practical tips, sales and most importantly how to align yourself with building audiences that go far beyond the public and into the spectrum of ideal clients.

Our Audience Attraction method has been likened to a platonic dating method for customers rather than love interests. It has been the backbone of what we have taught now to 100s of amazing entrepreneurs.

Don't build it so they will just magically arrive. Rig the entire game toward a gravitational field that pulls your audience into your atmosphere so that you can lovingly accept a stampede of super-eager fans supporting you and your business.

There is no overnight success and there is very rarely any "easy," "just happened" and "I hardly even noticed" sales either.

Everyone you look up to in the online space has stood where you are now. They have had to realise that audience building, lead generating, visibility and brand awareness are the well from which the entire business drinks. Without them, there is no you.

I am going to help shift your perspective so that you can understand how to come at this in a way that will be valuable to your audience, your business, and your life.

If it has taken you 40+ years to truly understand who you are, why do you expect to:

1. Learn how to communicate all the intricate parts of that in 1 /2/3/ 5 days?
2. Expect your audience to see it, comprehend and champion it in 6 months or less?

Some great things take time to get moving.

That doesn't mean it's not working.
That doesn't mean it's not worth it.

Keep at it tiger 🐅 💜 Lets dig in.

PROLOGUE

I wait nervously with bated breath and somewhat now sweaty palms. Although I have now done this many times, the nerves of a thousand plus people with their eyes, screens and most importantly their ears on me is never lost.

The truth is, this is what I wanted, what my business needed and everything I have worked to achieve.

Having these thousand people who are all in some sort of business transition, and who need my expertise and help has not been by chance.

Each seat has been filled with someone on my ideal client spectrum. Each person is valued and valuable to me and my business.

Each second that passes, while I read more comments of excitement that grow in my free Facebook group, I become innately aware of the hard work and yet a sense of ease, that each of these pretties came to be here, to hold what I have to say in high esteem, to take the time and my direction.

Each member of the Zoom meeting is eager to either learn, connect with, or buy from me. Even those who are here to watch what I do and attempt to steal it are welcome because they are about to learn that when you lean into your own authenticity, being you cannot be stolen, cloned, or copied.

The competition doesn't exist.

Did fancy lead magnets bring them here? No.
Did Facebook Ads lead them here? No.

Each member has learned of me by means of organic content, audience referral, collaboration, or direct connection.

No Hacks are required.

I open the Zoom meeting and begin the process of filtering each person in. "mute all" and then "Allow all."

Deep measured breaths and gratitude. The joy flows over me as I see familiar friendly faces as well as eager excited faces.

Women on a journey to chance their hand in life, to make their own fate. Women taking the internet and the world by the balls and squeezing tightly until they get what they want.

"I am delighted to be here with you tonight," I begin, reminding myself to smile on the outside as well as the inside, "I will be your Marketing Mentor for the evening,

Tonight let me explain to you how to use The Audience Attraction Method."

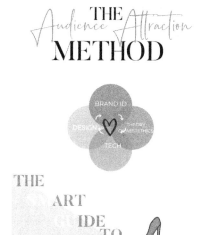

CHAPTER ONE
- IDENTITY AND
IDENTIFY

"Have you even lived if you haven't woken up in a cold sweat in the middle of the night gasping at the question "is this it?""

When it comes to Identity, we as humans talk a lot of smack. We discuss who we are and what we like and dislike to nearly anyone who will listen, quite often doing so to convince ourselves. The idea that you have to have this figured out in a solid concrete box by the end of your teenage years is the culture shift we never noticed shafted us and screwed us out of years of real self-discovery.

Self-discovery can happen any time, it can trigger after a dramatic event, it can linger in the wings gently all through your days like the breeze on your neck, gently reminding you of its presence. Sooner or later, you will figure out who you really are, or you won't, and the self-awareness of that will get you a surprising step closer anyway.

In those moments you will evaluate your lifestyle, your behaviours, your habits, your environments, relationships, health and often your career.

It doesn't matter if you are a seasoned business-owning pro, or a side hustle for fulfilment, turned "wait a minute, I can actually make real money from this!" All that matters is that now you know, you can't go back. We didn't always arrive here for self-development, did we? but we got it anyway! A bit like when you picked up this book thinking it was about "Marketing."

"It's life Jim but not as we know it."

When we start side hustles, businesses, partnerships, and adventures or even decide it's the appropriate time in our lives to begin that legacy, we do so thinking that the path we walk will be one of discovery in how we work or what we do as a career.

Many of us, if not all, didn't realise when we took the red pill that we were opening ourselves up to an awakening of self.

Self Awareness
Self Discovery
Self Mastery

Self Love
Self Acceptance
Self Transformation
Self Identification.

I start with Identity because it is often the part, we believe we know. The bit we are confident in, until we are not.

What if those behaviours you have, that feel set in stone are changeable? What if that environment you are in, is amendable? What if the version of you in your mind, when you are at your best, is achievable?

Pretty exciting right!??

The beautiful thing for you and I is that we don't ever have to put a full stop after who we are. We are an open paragraph that keeps being added to each day we ride this rock in outer space. We get to choose and we get to share where we are, exactly as we are, worthy of being seen, heard, and connected with, right now. Warts and all, you might say!

So many of us consider that to be visible in our businesses we need to show up in perfection. To fit some invisible bar of excellence that will make us worthy and worth watching, following, and listened to. The thing is, no matter your sector, your expertise, or the reason you want an audience, there is someone out there (usually a couple of hundred thousand actually) who want to see you. Want to hear you and are following, subscribing, or listening to someone else because they haven't been able to find you yet.

You find you, then you share you so that they can find you too.

Imagine your heart has a walking path on it, you will invite other souls to walk the path of your heart with you, but before you do you must walk it alone. Tread the track and set up the tiki torches and the flares that illuminate the way. Before we can invite others to walk with us, we have to illuminate the path. This is what I am going to show you in this book, but before you can illuminate the path, you must find the courage to take the steps by yourself, often into the unknown, into a darkness to walk it first and discover your own light.

If you are sat thinking "wow this is deep" for a book about marketing because I am starting to sound like a how-to-start-your-own cult guidebook then please bear with me. Some things are true for many things. Being followed by people is naturally going to contain some of the same things it would take to build a cult. But that is not why we are here!

If you think its deep; 1. You bet your ass it is, and 2. I promise it's all relevant. At no point will we be mentioning Kool Aid, shit! I just did!

One of the biggest things that will automatically turn off any kind of audience you are hoping to build is the host, leader, mentor, coach, influencer, CEO not having a clear sense of self. If you are an authentic human, you will inevitably have a wobble where you decide you don't know yourself well enough or you don't have confidence in yourself and perhaps you are not cut out for this path in life. This is encouraging to me; I want to know that you have explored that option and checked yourself before you wreck yourself!

Because that ability to self-evaluate clearly shows that you do in fact have what it takes.

The problem is a lot of the people you see online do not actually have the goods and they cannot check themselves too deeply because they have created a delusion and have bought into it with such commitment it would shatter their sense of self to be honest about who they are and what they want. So many are faking it till they make it. I call this the "fur coat and no knickers" syndrome and it's prevalent in coaches who must claim they made multiple 8 figures today whilst practising 5am Pilates with their healing drum and vibrational gongs and alchemy codes. P.s I love all those things, but them all together has a high percentage as a red flag.

It is in observing these people that you probably have determined you needed help to polish up. It is in these people your insecurities have gotten louder. Because that's their marketing tactic, misdirection both internally and externally. You don't have to decide to buy it, you don't have to have any negative feeling towards it. My loving suggestion is to be aware of what it does to your mindset and then just mosey on past it when you see it. It has no bearing on what you are doing or about to do.

What we are talking about is going to be different for you. It is a varied degree for us all. But the one constant is that you need to know who you were, you need to know where you stand right now and be honest about that location and you need to have some clarity on where you are going despite not actually being there yet. You get bonus points if you can tap into your personal power and believe you will become that person also, because belief is very important in what we have to do!

When the idea of manifestation was brought to me, I really liked it. I didn't immediately subscribe to it and I still don't believe if you think really hard you can poof magic things into your existence without actual actions to back it up. But I have seen enough mind magic to know that nothing moves out here until you move it in there first. The brain is a powerful tool, from which every action takes its first form. Even if you are more a child of science rather than that of the universe, it's hard to argue that all things come from the mind and the will to do something first.

Do you remember the movie "Kill Bill"? *"Wiggle your big toe."*

You didn't pick this book up without thinking it first. You didn't eat today without thinking first. You didn't sleep without thinking it first. When it comes to deciding who you are going to be today you need to decide, you need to "wiggle your big toe" and think it, and then action it after.

Thoughts + actions + direction = Your version of success.

Are you going to be the kind of person who gets up 20 minutes earlier to shower and has plenty of time to get ready in the morning? **don't be ridiculous** that's just our shared standard evening delusion! Ha, No seriously though ...YOU COULD BE!

The things we think become the actions we take and shape the life we lead. From small things to the big things, you have the power to reinvent yourself at any moment. To re-invent your life, your business and anything else for that matter!

You can wake up in the middle of the night in complete clarity and declare "I am the queen of money mindset" or "I will be the guiding light for women suffering menopause" or literally Whatever.The.Funk.You.Want!

The thing is, in the clarity of the moment when you see who you are becoming, what you want to be and all the things that lead you to this moment, you need to find peace and confidence in it. We will call this, your identity.

You see, in the world of psychology, identity is like a glittery disco ball at the centre of your personal dance floor. It's your sense of who you are, your personal unique pattern that leaves its mark like a cute lipstick smudge on the rim of your discarded Cosmo glass! It includes everything from your values, beliefs, goals and even the way you react when someone cuts you up in traffic. The nerve!

Why does this matter? Well, let me introduce you to Erik Erikson, a super smart dude in the field of psychology. He proposed this theory of psychosocial development (Erikson, 1963) where he suggests that our identity is formed throughout different stages of our lives. Imagine if you were playing hopscotch, but each square was a different stage of your life, and every hop was a challenge you had to face and overcome. A weird kind of fun, isn't it?

This lifelong game of hopscotch doesn't work like one we would know though, it's not linear and easy to follow, step by step. It is like real life, flowing backwards, catapulting forwards, sidewards and upwards and in a tangle too. It's often a mess and yet we move through the journey anyway.

Erikson's theory revolves around the idea that at each stage, a unique personal "crisis" or "trauma" must be resolved. If successful, it contributes to the formation of a healthy identity. If not resolved but held, it can result in a weak sense of self. A feeling of lack or unworthiness which can foster a level of self-sabotage in your subconscious.

Your main imaginary subliminal life opponent.

Imagine trying to pick an outfit without knowing what colours, styles, or patterns you like. Imagine trying to make key choices about how you want to live your life without truly knowing who you are, what you like, what you want? Pretty tricky Prettie!

You'd be in a bit of a pickle, wouldn't ya? You would feel a bit lost, wouldn't you? Perhaps a little unsure about your place or why you should be showing up for the world.

The thing is we are all to some degree a mirage of those who are around us, who shaped us. I love music because of my Father, I am into personal power, F the Patriarchy, and some rebellious feminine energies because of my sister Su. I am interested in legacy and teaching people things that enhance their life because of my sister Gillian. I have adopted things from friends, My husband Iain (we have a ton of things we no longer remember who introduced who to what that are now "ours") and this is how we live our lives.

Even in the pages of this book, older ideas will be shared and given in my way because the people who have taught, influenced, and challenged me have become part of me. This is okay! But you must own what the things are that you have picked up and made your own.

There will be other things that are just yours, such as for me. I can't stand ABBA. I feel sick that I even have given them a mention, but it's a good reference point as this particular personality identifier is all mine!

If you are not sure of who you are or who you are becoming, You may even ask the question:

"Why would they want to see me?"

Identity is so important in that it helps with that thing we all want a bit more of, and you need it when you are setting yourself up to be in front of others. To be seen as an expert, esteemed peer, or leader…. Drum roll please, in walks: self-esteem!

According to Rosenberg (1965) self-esteem is tied closely to our self-concept or identity. When you know who you are, it's like walking into a party in your favourite outfit. On the best day of your month, smelling like your favourite scent. Your make-up and hair are just right (even if you aren't wearing any) and you have a spring in your step. You feel confident, ready to take on the world and possibly even do the cha-cha slide!

Is that not what you sense within the confidence and energy of the people you follow and look up to online?

The thing is, a strong sense of identity can also protect against mental health issues as I learned with absolute shock and yet some delight when I trained to be a certified positive psychology coach. Research by Côté and

Schwartz (2002) suggests that individuals with a clear and consistent sense of identity might be less likely to experience anxiety and depression. It makes sense, right? Because what's on the inside and on the outside match and well...!

In a nutshell, your identity is like your own personal recipe. It's all the things that make you uniquely and brilliantly "YOU", and understanding it, is the secret ingredient to a happy and fulfilling life and an opportunity to be a shining light in the online world for others.

Knowing who you are is a foundational element to "showing up" that cannot be denied. It is the part which, if you cannot be sure of, or dare not look deeply into, you will not be able to communicate, support comprehension thereof, nor attract others alike.

Once you are able to SELF IDENTIFY and feel a level of conscious and subconscious comfort in this area, you are far more qualified to be able to identify who your ideal clients are and how and where to find them.

Now there is a chapter in this book called "Dreamy clients and where to find them," but in that part we are going to be a bit more action focused and practical. For the benefits of this part, I just want you to consider some key things.

What do you have in common with your ideal client?

What are your relatability points?

Are they like you? Any past versions of you? Are you wanting to spare them pain or a lesson you have had to live through or are you simply able to provide something for them that either solves a problem or brings them joy?

All of this is relevant in knowing how to show up for them and to do so in a way that honours... you guessed it - self.

It would be easy of me to ask you what your core values are. What are the things that really mean something to you? But for many of us, we only have a surface level understanding of ourselves in this way - often never truly knowing how to even scratch that surface deeper.

I adore a website called https://www.viacharacter.org/ that allows you to take a quiz that will identify your values in action. The answers may come out differently than you imagine, but you will likely be able to stem the answers back to reasons within you that make total sense, even if not glaringly obvious.

You see, when you decide what you share online you are going to consider all these things. You are going to want to execute your values, you are going to want to communicate who you are and what you believe in. You are going to want to know what is relatable to your audience so you can share it.

For instance, I could share that in between the last paragraph and this I had to stop. I took my son to bed, I put a clothes wash on, folded the drying, washed the pots, ordered Jack back to bed once more and made a de-caff coffee (far too late for full cafe now) before sitting back down to this chapter.

Why would I share that with you?

Well,

1. It's honest.

2. If you have kids, grandkids, animals, a partner, a house, pots, laundry, or coffee you just related to me.

Even if none of those are relevant, you just got a little slice of my world in your head. You have imagined me standing at my sink or sipping my coffee. Now that is a shared relatability.

You either understood me because of the parts of life we share and it spoke to a part of you or you feel like you know me better, which you do. It's all relevant.

Takes one to know one.

Takes knowing oneself to attract another one.

CHAPTER TWO
- BLOCKS

So, throughout the time I was teaching audience attraction, and more importantly (I guess), or working with a full range of different wonderful people. I noticed that in regard to showing up and being visible, whilst having the impact that you want to have for an audience, there is a massive thing that needs to be addressed.

Before we can even really get into the nitty gritty, we need to address something that is powerful in terms of return. I want you to understand what you may need to do next so that we don't deny that there is a lot more to building an audience than just the practical actions, just the practical strategy. There's a lot of emotional "stuff" that's included in this as well. We look at this chapter as a starting off point. But might need to come back to this theme and to this chapter semi regularly throughout your journey, perhaps regularly throughout your entrepreneurial career.

What I want you to know, is the reason why this is important to me; that we get this out of the gate straightaway, is because this is a loving space for you. Between the pages of this book there is a safe space for you to think and feel and address things that you probably didn't think would be included in a book such as this. There are going to be moments throughout these chapters where you question my point, probably .

You have bought this book to build an audience you can nurture, to get clients, you've come to me for lots of reasons that are very good strategic business reasons because you know I can help you.

Even with all my expertise, experience, and acumen I cannot help you to be able to shine and show a part of yourself that you perhaps haven't been able to show before, without some digging. We need to go a bit deeper into who you are, what you're dealing with and what your blocks, personal and visibility, may be. We're going to take those blocks that we perhaps have naturally, and we're not going to let them stop us from what we want to achieve okay?!

We're going to use them to catapult us into a different perspective and into a different arena. You are not alone in being apprehensive about being visible.

There's a little bit of mindset work that goes into this, actually, that's an understatement.

But there's also a little bit of; understanding your emotional state, understanding your personal circumstances, and having a good understanding of your environment. We need to focus on what things you have around you that may be hindering rather than helping your opportunities to be visible and show up. Your opportunities to connect with an audience, your opportunities to get on out there and be consistent are built on this foundation.

So, with that in mind, it would be remiss of me not to have a little disclosure, at this part of the book, a bit of a disclaimer, that this chapter, when you embrace it may unveil some deeper emotional issues that require support outside of these pages.

I'm not a therapist, I am a positive psychology coach and marketing expert only. There is no doctorate here. You can lay a lot of responsibility on me and I will be here for you, I will support you. But I'm not, I can't say this word, a clinician, I'm not in the medical profession.
Be aware that if this chapter brings something up to you, that may include recognising any past emotional trauma, that if you need any assistance in your wellbeing, that we are lovingly going to suggest that you seek medical and professional advice in that arena without delay.

If this will knock on something that's a little bit deeper, then please do consider that for yourself.

It is important that you can be completely honest and vulnerable here with yourself, without judgement, without shame. If only we were beings that did not need to be reminded not to judge or shame ourselves! But alas we are not, so there is your reminder. Throw that inner critic out and give yourself the gift of compassion!

Here we go!

The Veil

So, let's first talk about the veil. Whether you realise it or not, at some point, when you made the decision to be a business, you will have adopted or recognised the veil in others and attempted to put one on yourself. The veil is a term that I came up with in my company and teach our Certified Social Media Managers, to describe that feeling of showing up in recognition, when you realise that in order for you to have a business or to fulfil your dreams, your purpose, and get out there, that you're actually going to have to show up a little bit. Often the veil is when you realise that perhaps you want to show up in a more polished type of way.

The veil allows us to filter ourselves somewhat and sometimes we use it to hide. We can hide behind lots of different things. We can hide behind the brand tone in our emails, we can hide behind the look of our website, we can hide behind our branding, we can hide behind specific personality factors; I hid behind my eyelashes for a long, long time. Still do sometimes.

You can create this kind of feeling that you need an additional persona or maybe even like a different kind of Avatar version of yourself, for you to be comfortable being visible. If you've ever felt or ever thought to yourself, Okay, when I show up on a live, I'm going to be really professional, I'm going to want it to look like my house is neat and I am in a fancy office. I am going to wear this top or have my make up like... *(insert online guru here)*.

Now that I have mentioned this, have you ever come up

against that kind of resistance; of there being a veil? The need to look a certain way so that people, "think I know what I'm talking about", at all?

If you are sat nodding at your book right now or even allowing a well-timed "Hmm humm" escape your lips, then know that you are a natural normal human consumer who has been affected by mainstream media and advertising. Congratulations! You have just been initiated into my world of "pretties" – Welcome!

Online, in adverts and in magazines we are shown things a certain airbrushed, best foot forward kind of way. It is called marketing and pre mid 2000's it was the ONLY cool way to do things. But things have changed. We however are still making ourselves comfortable with those changes.

If you were to break down my veil, go on I will let you, there are lots of things that I at the very very beginning of my journey used to do. That gave me a little bit of confidence but also stopped me a little bit in terms of really connecting.

We have this idea that everything must be very positive. That it can't show what real life is about. Perhaps we must hide that REAL isn't always positive.

We can think "I have to be a certain type of person to do this." It is connected to our self-esteem.

I want to introduce you to the two types of self-esteem.

Contingent self-esteem. Based on the approval of others or on social comparisons.

Certain events will shape one's self-esteem when the

individual bases their self-worth on the outcome of those events. [1] The success or failure of any situation can result in fluctuations of an individual's self-esteem. [2] A manifestation of someone with contingent self-esteem is excessive self-consciousness. Such excessive self-consciousness, as occurs with contingent self-esteem, involves extreme criticism of one's self, concern of how they are perceived by their peers, and feelings of discomfort in social settings.(source - wiki)

Non contingent self-esteem. Basically, the type that doesn't give two flying flamingos about anyone else's approval and is secure in itself, without the need for external validation. (Source - well, me)

For instance, complete disclosure here, my life's had its difficulties. My relationships sometimes struggle. I've had family that are in hospital, my kids get sick, sometimes they are grumpy and tired and sometimes they just want mum to stop working. I still go and pick them up from school, although sometimes my life looks like Michelle Pfeffier in the movie "One fine day," at how frantically I am trying to hold everything together. You could have a right good giggle at my situation at any given moment because for all you know, my life and business would look perfect when in fact my world is burning around me. That would be the veil.

When these things have happened, have I shown that online? in my emails? and throughout my videos? Would I dare come on and say, actually, this is what I'm going through?

You'd see now that you know that I have, but I have done so still with a little veil.

When we have these things going on, we might think, Oh, I can't show the world that because they will think less of me.

But think about it. Say you join me on an Instagram live this week; If I say, "this week, I'm having the week from hell", would you really think me any less professional? No! Those things are not mutually exclusive, sometimes we aren't perfect, that does not mean we are any less than anyone else and it certainly doesn't mean we are not capable!

Those things we worry about. What people think about us in our honesty and vulnerability don't matter to how capable you are and what people really want to see from you.

In fact, if I was to put a post out right now and say, by the way guys, "I am having a really hard time right now in my personal life," I know that would be one of my best performing posts.

People generally are good and they care. People generally are lovely and get invested, they want us to be happy.

But we don't trust that. so we create little veils to hide behind, "people will think I'm not good enough," "people will think I can't do it."

For a moment, give yourself a pause here. Don't forget to bookmark or fold a little square in the corner. Give yourself an opportunity to think about things that you might be telling yourself,

"Oh, I couldn't possibly share that."
"I shouldn't admit I'm not feeling well today."

"I can't admit I've had financial difficulties in the past."
"I won't tell them I struggle with social anxiety."

You don't have to tell anyone about the things that come up for you. Those things belong to you to do what you want with them. But let's be aware of them and strip them of their power.

Exercise: A good exercise for this would be to write down some of the things you believe you shouldn't admit publicly to your audience. Get them down on paper and then do two things. 1. Re write positive statements on another piece of paper that flip the perspective.

"I can't admit I made no sales in my last launch," turns into, "If I was to share that I made no sales in my last launch it would make no difference to my potential to make sales in the future." You could add a little star * next to the ones that you might even feel comfortable sharing one day in the future. Then burn the original negative list - bye bye inner critic and self-criticism!!

That's what we're gonna do with all those little feelings that forced us to make Veils to hide beneath, we're going to shift the perception. That doesn't mean you are going to show up on camera without your lashes (could you imagine? eek) or tell people about your last loose bowel movement. You still get to filter out what you share, but you get to have the second kind of self-esteem about it. About all of it. Behind closed doors where it matters. Between you and well, you.

I don't want you to ever lay everything out just for the sake of it to the public either. That's not what I'm asking you to do. But I'm going to support you in finding the power in yourself, so that you are not scared to share the things and so YOU can decide how, when, and why without the hiding.

It ties into the belief "I'm good enough." I want you to look after that belief in yourself better than you have ever looked after a houseplant. It needs constant attention. You should sing to it. Self-esteem loves it when you sing to it!

I would love you to say the following statement (in your head if you want but there is power in your vocal cords vibrating this).

"It's gonna work out for me."

Even when going through a bit of a tough personal time I am selective about which bits of my story to share, and you have the power to do the same but sans the fear.

You may have reasons, in the form of humans you care about, being the block to the honest.

So many people worry about not sharing their light, because of somebody else who perhaps, would be affected by it.

You may not want your parents, friends, children, or ex's to know things that your ideal client would like to know and would relate to. Not to mention the unadulterated pleasure of having total freedom to express one's self.

Or it could be a factor such as your status or age.

Your ideal client might want somebody who's your age and experience level, they may connect to the fact that you were in care or have a criminal record. You might think I am going too far but we are human beings and we have a whole wealth of experiences and some of them won't be what you would see on the cover of Vogue magazine.

The things we do decide to share that may look negative can turn into a total positive for someone who is looking to relate.

Human and human connection, the relatability.

When we are magnetic, we are magnetic to people not because of what we have, but because of what's in them and what they have experienced and what is in us and what we have experienced. Our people are going to relate to us, that's because there's a commonality.

People don't come to me and go "Dawn is brilliant. I'm going to work with Dawn because Dawn is brilliant and perfect and never has any problems."

They refer me to their friends and business associates with a simple "she made me feel something that's important and that I am important."

All I do is mirror back your genius to you, and yet you relate to me,

It's really important that we know that about our people and find the right way to share that in a way that's comfortable for us.

Let me tell you about "She." So, this person, "she" wants her clients to know she can be trusted. "She" wants to build the Know, Like and Trust. "She" knows her ideal clients and wants to connect. "She" wants to make regular sales, which of course is the backbone of all these things that we're trying to do. And "she" also wants social proof and testimonials. "She" wants to be able to host a group where she can have that great opportunity for connection to flourish. But "She" has all these blocks too, very similar to what we've spoken about today.

Are you, "she"?

If so then we may need to rearrange the blocks that might be coming up for you.

I use the term universal to represent a general and globally seen thing, as in, this is highly likely to happen to most humans.

Very regular, it's very general, lots of people will have felt the same way.

Then on top of these universal blocks we get to have our own set of personal blocks, which is lovely. Aren't we all lucky?!

We have our own unique personal collection of stuff as well. There are certain things that we will all feel together and there's certain things that will be just us.

This is a self-awareness test. This is an opportunity for us to bring what might be in our subconscious into our conscious, and because we can't work with it when it's on autopilot, we must bring it to the surface so we can consciously flip our perspectives in a positive way.

Have you ever felt this way? (*feel free to doodle your answers here*) ...

*They will judge me. (I'd like you to pay particular attention to who "they" are).

*What will people think?

*I'm not good enough.

*I can't do this, everyone's going to notice that I'm fraud.

These are tough ones to bring out.

This chapter is the elephant in the room for so many online personalities. We're all in it together here, rather than ignore it. Let's decorate the elephant. Let's recognise it, let's bring it to our conscious and be aware of it so that it's not a block if we say it's not.

"But what about people who actually DON'T, WON'T like me and will see all my vulnerability," I hear you silently whisper to the part of yourself that is still afraid. They will live on and so will you.

If you knew of me before you decided to Amazon Prime this book, the chances are, you are, 1. A prettie who likes me, enjoys my content, and wanted more, or even just to support me. Or 2. You are part of my version of "The I hate Rachel Green club" and you are here to see what I am saying and keep tabs on what you know about me.

Hello Hater Taters!

Not everyone likes me *SHOCK HORROR* and that's cool. Not everyone will like you either. "Their problem! I think your wonderful!"

Thing about NON contingent self-esteem is that it doesn't care what they think, remember? Because although we want people to like us, our worth doesn't depend on it anymore.

Another Veil we use is that there is no place for us. Have you ever felt it is too noisy online?

"Every time I open my Facebook, there's somebody who does what I do shouting about what they're doing. And why would anybody want to work with me?"

This is a BLOCK feeling. It often comes with a couple of block like friends such as "I don't want to contribute to the noise."

It can make you feel like backing away! So often when we get this particular feeling, we'll open our phone, we'll read a few things and think I'm not going to post. You might think "I'm just gonna come away from that."

You may feel like it's time to back off. Only Comment when relevant perhaps. This is why it's a block.

Because it's okay to have an opinion that it's noisy. It's okay to look at that swimming pool and think there's not an inch there that I can dive into. But it's not okay to walk away back to the changing rooms and get your clothes back on. What I want you to do is jump in, make the move, I want you to bomb into that pool anyway!

What you don't realise is everyone watches you run up and goes, "damn, I need to make some space here." "She's about to bomb into this pool." "If I don't move, she's gonna land on my head."

Right? Recognise that there is room for you.

That is what I want us to get used too. Yes, it's noisy, but it's "your" noise! Because it wouldn't be just more noise! "Your" noise is just as valuable, just as worthy, if not more so, than all the hustle and bustle that you've got on your screen.

We're not backing away. We're elbowing our way in - unapologetically. But we're also not going to do what most people do, which is the song and the dance, and edited and everybody looked at me! Because that is not how you cultivate proper attention. You can cultivate temporary, loud attention, hype that way, but long-term attention, consistent attention is cultivated in a much calmer, much more confident space.

When I was about 11, I got the opportunity to go to my first ever drama masterclass with my best friend Katie. We were really fired up to be training with a lady who was pretty famous at the time. Jacqui Leonard, she had been in loads of soaps and she was really friendly but totally famous to our little class.

Off we went to this masterclass and followed all the drama games and listened as she delivered wisdom about auditions and confidence and nerves. At one point she put three of us to a task for everyone to watch. The brief was simple, "I want you to get our attention, the three of you are going to perform at the exact same time and I want you to demand attention."

There was no direction, she didn't tell us what she wanted us to do.
Earlier for something else she had given me her jacket. She said "Action" and away we went. I knew exactly what I would do. I took her jacket off and I was swinging the jacket around and I was throwing it up in the air and frantically throwing out my arms and legs and swinging this jacket (which she wasn't very happy with me about afterwards). I got carried away with performance trying desperately to demand attention.

There was another girl next to me and she was like all singing and dancing as well. And then the third girl who obviously had got a lot more drama experience than us both, had chosen a different approach. She sat and she very delicately and slowly peeled an imaginary banana. Shortly after she made herself an imaginary cup of tea, slowly, meticulously whilst being totally invested in the mime and the details thereof. At the end, they explained to us that the vast majority didn't even see me swing the jacket. They couldn't care less. They were watching the quiet, the calm, the consistent, the meticulous, the confident girl. She was captivating in all of her "I don't need to volley for your attention" energy, "I'm good here, regardless of if you see me," is a massive message. It's a massive vibe. "I'm here regardless of whether you're watching."

It breaks through the noise. We may have to elbow our way in, but then we're going to captivate, we're going to confidently steal attention, but not in the way that you might think we're going to. We're going to attract not chase. That's what this is all about. This is why you're here.

Another block you may not see coming is the one where you are secretly scared to succeed. I had an excellent conversation with a mindset expert, who I adore. And she explained to me the fear of success, the fear of what if I succeed comes from our innate desire to understand our own identity.

For instance, every now and then when I'm teaching, a Northern twang in my voice will come out. I might tell you about my childhood and some of the stories that include lessons. They often paint a very, very sad, lonely, and quite poor child that grew up in one of the worst areas of the UK. Where I grew up is one of the most deprived towns in the UK and looking at me now, working with thousands of amazing people, and being able to provide value almost doesn't make sense to a little girl who started life that way.

You may not be able to put those two things together.

Perhaps you feel like being successful feels like being a fake. Maybe you think striving to be a better version of yourself, feels like you're a little bit too big for your boots.

"Who do I think I am?"

When you look at me, if you think, "how did this person who started up in this situation at the early stages of her life, end up here?" You could be overlooking that these things have shaped me but not defined me.

The version of you that is happy, successful, and bright may also have been shaped by times that don't make much sense to who you are right now or more importantly who you are becoming. But they cannot define you or make your path any less worthy. Success won't change you. Only you can change you.

You can be aware of the questions:

"What happens?"
" Who will that person be?"

What limiting beliefs are you carrying around about yourself when it comes to that success?
It could be as simple as:

"I don't think I'll be as kind to people when I have money and success." or "I don't think I'll have as much time for people anymore."

"I think when I have the means to do whatever it is I want to do, I might put myself first and that changes how I see myself."

"I might not be the person who turns up to Mary's house first, on the weekend with flowers every weekend, I might be the person who is too busy jetting off somewhere actually living a life."

Getting what you want can be an identity conflicting thing. So be honest with yourself about that.

Lots of things come from the consumption of media, not necessarily the things we are putting out into the world but the stuff that we're consuming.

You may have more bespoke and unique personal circumstances, maybe you have people who you've left behind or family members that you have issues with? People who don't support you, the people who don't understand you, the people who don't really get what it is that we're doing here.

These situations will also contribute to those blocky feelings. It's good to be aware, the data sources, and your brain will tell you time and time again:

"No, it's not worth opening Pandora's box, it's not worth sharing my light."
"It's not worth posting about this real thing. It's not worth me being honest, I'll just put a shiny, separated distance post out instead, so that no one can ever get close to me, no one can ever judge me, and no one can ever call me out on it."

I want you to think of those data sources, I want you to think about where you are, in terms of sharing your light, because all this previous media, and I say previous, it's still in circulation. Still! But it doesn't have the same power for you.

This is a moment for you to declare your own power to change. Because believe it or not, we are the media. There's only one way for us to have an impact on all of this. And that's for us to decide that we're going to overthrow it. And for us to overthrow it, we must do things a different way, we must get past those blocks. And we must recognise that we're not one of these people at the bottom of the pyramid consuming all the media from somebody, we're actually the star at the top of the pyramid, putting our message out to the masses.

I'm not talking to you about how many likes you get, how many comments you get, or how many people are physically watching your videos when you're on a live, we're going to remove the worry about that for the moment.

I'm talking about your mindset when you show up. I'm talking about you showing up to the live today, even though you've done five in a row and nobody came. I'm talking about you feeling like you have the power to make changes in what media is out there and being consumed for your people in your niche.

Are you there for your ideal clients? Are you there for your people? Or not. You have the power.

I want you to imagine, you walk into a room, there's two doors, on the left-hand side is the door where you decide that you are going to influence people in your positive way. And you're going to shine your light.

Through the other door, you get to be a consumer. You get to decide that you're not going to contribute and you're not going to put yourself in that place to be a leader.

Mentally visualise yourself walking through the door on the left.

Because you are a leader now, there are new rules. You are not allowed to abandon your power for pride or ego or fear. You have to show up for the people you are going to help and they are above you in priority.

We're going to overcome these blocks so that you can be the authority you naturally are. You're going to be the lead; you're not going to have time to consume and worry about what other people are doing. Because you're going to be the trailblazer, you're going to be the one that's consistent for your people, you're going to turn up regardless.

You're okay, because you recognise these digital opportunities that we have in front of us, they're just tools. They are just tools for us to share our light.

The data sources will still be there. So, my darlings, you do have to protect yourself in terms of recognising things in your environment that may knock you off your stride. That's why it is important we recognise this now, before we go deeper.,

It is very likely that we are all going to need to keep coming back to this.

You can reject some of the narratives that somebody else gave you, I lovingly invite you to say that to yourself out loud or in your head.

"I can reject the narratives that somebody else gave me."

Practical tips for personal movement of narratives that you've adopted, that weren't your own.

You can meditate.
You can use affirmations.
Lean on your support networks (if not already in my free group, come and join us)
Seek professional help.
You can get support in past trauma healing.
Invest in self-belief practitioners.
Practice gratitude is a brilliant one.
Accept praise.

We're gonna flip some of the things we've talked about on the head. "I'm not good enough" is the feeling and the reason behind it is because of natural imposter syndrome.

Here's a little-known fact about impostor syndrome from the amazing Dunning Kruger effect and Theory.

The bottom 25% of any skill overestimate themselves the most. The fact that you're invested in learning something you may not think you are good at, is enough to prove you're probably not an impostor. The bottom 25% probably will never buy this book.

The cute thing about this, is if you have ever felt like an imposter, you immediately cancel out your chances of being an impostor. Because guess what people who aren't imposters do? They check themselves. They self-regulate, they make sure that they have the goods because they're not happy being an imposter. They don't want to fake it. They want the real stuff. You've decided to learn things you don't know. It automatically discounts you from being an imposter.

So, when you have that moment of, "oh," "you're gonna find out I'm not good enough for this." You must go, "wait a minute, wait a minute. I have worked really hard. And I check myself regularly and am constantly making sure that I am doing the right thing. I'm constantly learning new things. I'm doing business in a good way. I've put business as a focus. How could I possibly be seen as an imposter when I am doing the right things? I'm not an imposter. I'm not faking it. This is real."

Remove that feeling. Remove that thought.

What will people think, is a thought that is born from ego! Ego tries to protect us; ego doesn't mean to be such a pain in the tush. It tries to protect us but sometimes it gets in the way.

You can overcome that by thinking about how you help people. To remember that the people you are showing up for, are more important than what the people who you don't help think of you.

For instance, I could have a massive block in writing this book. I might get worried about sharing something, thinking about the bully from high school who's recently been stalking my Instagram. I could think about her and stop. The embarrassment and the fear from the 12-year-old fragile girl still inside me, could still be a bit scared, a bit conditioned to reduce herself. To stay small.

The way I overcome this; is instead I'm thinking about you. I'm thinking about pretties. I'm thinking about the frustration you feel when you want to get your business out there and don't know how. I am thinking about you highlighting parts, making notes, nodding to my ideas. I am thinking about that "aha" moment when you get something from this book that relates just to you. Because you are more important than my fears, you are more important than my ego. If this book fails horrendously and I am embarrassed off the worlds stage then that's okay. You are worth the risk.

The best comment I ever get on my content is "I needed this today."

There is no higher compliment and that comment is what I do it for. When you recognise how important you, dear reader are to me, also consider how important your soon to be audience is to you. They should be very high on your priority list.

Ego is trying to protect you, so don't feel bad about it, but be aware of it, reduce it a bit and practice putting it lower on the list of important things. Then one day remove it entirely.

You may also need to overcome the learned practices that others have put before you. Practices steeped in logic that you may have adopted. Such as lowering your position to be respectful to others who are louder. Remember the captivation of a mimed cup of tea and that your voice is equally or even more important. Try not to care what "they" think, what "you" think, matters. What your "ideal clients" think, matters.

This is probably a good time to recognise that whoever "they" are to you - they are not your ideal clients, they're not the established relationships you have created whilst becoming part of the entrepreneurial community. They likely don't affect your income positively or negatively. This is a good reason to emotionally detach from "them."

It matters to the people who will work with you in the future. It matters to the people who you're working with right now. It matters to the people that you've met, that you networked with, that have been on previous courses with you, that sometimes check in on you on social, that join different groups with you, that join different challenges with you. It matters to them.

The reason for these blocks are often a safety response, fear of failure, fear no one's interested. Can you find a way to recognise that the level of threat is really low? You are not a tasty deer, in the wilderness close to a hungry lion. If Sharon from down the road thinks you're getting a bit too big for your boots, will it really matter?

When there is no real threat, cut off your safety response and allow your opportunity factor to take its place. Because even if you did all the things, and people don't immediately show up, it won't mean something about you personally, and if you know that it doesn't, then it's a situation where nobody, nobody can hurt you.

You'll be okay. I know it gets emotional because it feels personal. It's about the only thing that isn't.

You think "They don't want to hear from me." I am telling you, lovingly - You're not qualified to make that choice for your audience. Only your audience can decide that. You can tell yourself this and allow it to stop you in your tracks but it won't make it any truer.

100%, you cannot say what your audience is interested in or not, until you have got yourself out there, and I mean over and over for months and months.

We've got things we know will interest our audience, and you'll learn and you'll create topics that you can rely on to work. With practice that's no problem. The problem is the belief in yourself that you can.

When you are posting, going live, emailing, and doing all the things, you look to why your audience didn't show up as a bad thing. What if they didn't show up today, for lots of different reasons? You can't say it's because they're not interested when you don't know that.

Say it out loud or to yourself:

"I'm not qualified to decide that my audience isn't interested in what I have to say."

You've sat here bravely and have considered what your blocks are, and you may have realised some are specific to your life only and some are those that we all suffer in varying degree.

You have explored the feeling of "what if no one is interested in me."

So, I'd like to introduce you to a lady called "Bread face." Bread face is easy to look up on Instagram, Tik Tok, or YouTube as she has made an entire career out of smashing her beautiful face into bread (yes, the food) and cakes on camera.

That's right, my darling friends. Bread face is a very successful, multi-millionaire entrepreneurial woman and every bakeries worst nightmare.

She smooches her face into baked goods on camera and then shares those videos. Every single time you have a wobble and you think to yourself, no one's going to want to hear / see anything I have to offer, I want you to think of Breadface.

Go and SMOOSH your own face in some bread if you need to as a reminder. Whatever works! Make it a ritual if you need too but remember there's a random lass out there in the world, making millions using Warburtons as her beauty routine.

I love a, "If they can do it, so can you", story. Trust me when I say out of 4.8 billion people there will be some who want to know about what you have to speak about.

A few years ago, I was at a networking type event and I was utterly energetically exhausted but I managed some conversation with a lovely woman who wanted to pick my brains about Instagram. She was convinced her ideal clients were not on there, convinced there was no point in trying to use the platform, despite her niche being perfect for that side of the internet.

At the time there was 1 billion active users (there's more now) so I asked her "How many clients do you need in your business to earn what you want this year?" Her answer was fourteen.

Fourteen. I said, probably a bit too directly, "You don't think you can find fourteen people in a billion who will be interested in what you have to say and want to buy from you?"

Months later I spoke to this lovely lady again and she recalled the conversation back to me. I had forgotten it in the haze of exhaustion (from my in-person social battery failing me quite horrendously) on the day. She explained she had quit her job and gone for it, she had clients and she was doing well. What I had said had fired her up, motivated her. I was absolutely delighted!

She is still thriving and growing and recently launched her own book, her client list is many multiples of 14!

If breadface doesn't convince you, look up Nico avocado a millionaire seven times over. Nico records himself eating and putting on weight. He started off at a healthy weight. He no longer is. It's a dangerous business for sure and you are probably thinking it's ludicrous. It is. That is my point. What you want to share probably is more needed, more mainstream, more interesting than you could ever imagine.

I'm showing you this ridiculousness. Not because I'm trying to introduce you to the school of ridiculous online businesses. I'm reminding you of how worthy you are, of what value you provide regardless of your niche.

If these people can make millions of pounds of these businesses, we can find you the humans for your audience to make your business a success.

One last one, Bell Delphine! Bell Delphine sells her bath water for 30 pounds a tiny tub and earns a fortune. At the time of writing this book she's made more than $1.5 million from selling her bathwater.

I want you to think about these people and I want you to consider what Bella thinks about trolls or people who don't agree with her business. I'll bet Bella couldn't give two hoots whilst she takes herself to the bank to buy literally anything she wants.

Nasty public and keyboard warriors and trolls for someone with that sized audience are expected. But what you make them mean about you and your business is up to you.

Trolls are another fear-based block. They give us the fear of public humiliation. Trolls are inevitable.

What do you think successful people think of trolls? Do you think they care? Whilst they're laughing all the way to the bank? Do you think these guys care about trolls whilst they're buying their multimillion-pound apartments in beautiful locations of the world? Do you think they care about trolls when they're waking up at 11 o'clock on a Tuesday and they don't have to do any work today and they're going to go and take all their loved ones to brunch in the sunshine.

They don't care. Neither should we. Trolls are inevitable. As soon as you become visible, you will see them. Remember that if you do ever fall subject to a troll, they boost engagement with an excellence of no other. If they start a conversation, they boost engagement. If they add to the conversation, they boost engagement! If you find your audience comes to defend you - guess what, another boost of engagement!

As long as you can manage your emotions well enough to not take it personally and react, then you are all good.

I love the idea that this book will debunk the myths about what constitutes getting audience building right. I also want you to know that there is a sweeping scale of wrong, and that most of anything that you try to do to get your business more attention wouldn't even register on that scale. So, you don't have to worry about that anymore. I'm just going to pluck that worry out of your brain because it no longer exists. Okay?! Pluck and we throw it into the wind!

Nothing you could do could ever be that wrong as long as you are remaining true to your ethics and values whilst you do it.

Competitors as a block

This is an interesting one because so many of us look at others doing similar things and decide that we shouldn't bother doing something because someone already did. Could you imagine if we looked at the rest of life this way. "I won't brush my teeth; Sandy already did that." "I won't bother getting married, there has been a wedding this year." You do what you need to do for you, why does anyone else even come into the picture?

There have been times when my "competitors" have come to me, of course, in the belief that opportunities can be stolen. They've felt sore about those contracts I have been able to secure and made it mean something about them. It doesn't, it didn't and it never could.

What is meant for me cannot be taken, and I don't want what is meant for you. There is enough for us all.

Overcoming this block comes from cultivating a deep faith in your opportunities that only you can deliver what you're offering in the way you deliver it. Practice the opportunity of openness, if "competitors" (I prefer the term peers) come along and "copy" then be grateful for the flattery and the brand boost.
I can't tell you how many people have come to me because somebody else has offered what I'm offering. Then they looked deeper, have done their due diligence and found the breadcrumb back to the originator. If they don't do that and they work with the other person, trust that there was a reason that works for them in doing so.

People who don't work with me will get good results working with others. I am not the only connection specialist on the globe and thank goodness! There aren't enough of us in my opinion. I am grateful for the others in my niche working well and fighting the good fight. Together we are supporting people in a great way!

Gratitude and the belief that the right people for you will

find you, (as long as you aren't hiding behind a brick wall of blocks, determined not to be found), the way in which you cultivate this energy will be everything.

How about the fear of commitment? You are signing yourself up to post publicly, regularly from now for forever - how does that sit in your gut?

For those who have this block, It all feels a bit too much to commit. There's a lack of understanding and comfort in executing the task. The strange thing about this worry, is the denial that the commitment to business has already been made. If you're in business, you've invested in your business, you're already here, right now.

I'm afraid you're already in it. So, we can't take it away unless you have decided that you are going to quit. The commitment to be there for your audience is already there. The use of visibility practices and social media is no longer a "nice to have." It is a staple of what is bare minimum requirements to keep afloat and thrive.

But we understand that the feeling isn't really commitment, and reframe it as what it is, which is overwhelm. From that understanding we can make the task more efficient so we don't suffer that drowning feeling. If you still feel this way in the future, you can always outsource the task.

The great thing about focusing on audience building is the journey is simple in the main part.

Audience = Leads = Clients /Customers

So, if you focus on getting past these blocks whilst in build mode, you will naturally at some point gain paying clients who will support you in having a budget to outsource these tasks to!

Part of the power of overcoming blocks, is you're going to take back ownership of what success looks like for you by addressing them. Don't hide from your demons, learn their names, find out what makes them tick, and then starve them of it until they wither and slip away. Wow, that got a bit dark! Sorry...

Recognise that you choose who you become and how you attain success. You're not going to turn into the scary mean lady who doesn't have friends or family because she has lots of money instead. It won't change you unless you let it, unless that was already in you. Give yourself permission, earn what you want to earn, whether that's 500 pounds a month, 5000 pounds a month or 5 million. You decide, okay?!

You also don't have to sort all of this out in your head by the end of this book or even in six months from now. You only have to organise your thoughts about the next few steps, each in its own time.

What I wish for you is the type of success that creeps up on you. You put in the time and focus and then one day you wake up and go to your very own content studio, to serve a mass of amazing women who want to work with you. To be financially stable and luxury level secure. To go on holiday, to have a team if you want to, to have the flexibility to work anywhere in the world. Okay so I am using myself as an example, but remember the, "If I can do it, so can you."

I did it, I am doing it and I love my job and I'm excited

nearly every single day to do it.

This type of success is what happens for you when you choose what works for you and cultivate your own autonomy.

These blocks and any that you have recognised in yourself that are not listed here do not define you or your opportunity for growth unless you allow them too.

The only power they have is what you allow. Throw out the rules prettie - this is YOUR show. For instance, a chapter in a book shouldn't really go over 8,000 words and as I type I am adding more to my massive word count. I could care - or I could remember this is MY book and you having the information is more important than an invisible rule. I say, "stuff it" and do whatever the franklin I want. You can do the same!

CHAPTER THREE - MEET THE PLAYERS

A Birds eye view

When you're an entrepreneur in business, and, or a solopreneur, quite often you're making decisions from a driving seat, which is an individual or solo perspective. Even if you have a team or business partners, quite often, they're only making their decisions based on what they can see as well. There is absolutely nothing wrong with this but it causes the humble entrepreneur a little more stress in trying to figure out what platforms may be best for them to spend their time on. As I write this, I know I am in a really really privileged position. And when I say privileged, I mean ridiculously so in a way that we are entirely grateful for every single day.

We have 1000s of records of client data, all working with us in different ways across the digital scope. We have a really good landscape of what's working and what's happening in digital sales at any given time. That information is quite easy to measure within most given industries and this is why I want to share that view, with you.

A lot of the statistics in this chapter are simple statistics that you could find in many places out there in the world. However, the data that we've collected within the statistics, is information that we've been able to gather through our platform, through our privileged point of view and through our pretties. Which means that we can give you a bird's eye view rather than a solo individual direct perspective, on exactly what's happening in terms of social media profiles, platforms, and visibility as a doing word, and that is why I include it for your lovely eyes and brains. Review it and take the relevant parts like your favourite picky tea plate at an all you can eat buffet.

I often shy away from anything that could be seen as "general advice or information" because if you can google it, why would you need to hear or read it from me? But then I wonder, perhaps the perspective wouldn't be the same without somebody shedding that light in this way, within the chapters of a book like this. So here we are, you and me, we might as well address it.

Often when I deliver this information, I have to update it each time. No two presentations are the same and no two can comfortably sit within the timeframe I have given them, (usually an hour or so and we will almost always go over by 40 minutes). That is because this information, albeit on one level generic is also the missing information so many of my clients need, when they are making informed choices about their content. We, as flawed humans, so quickly jump to the, "is it me?" questions, we often look past, ignore, or neglect the data in front of us.

With this chapter we shouldn't just trust our gut and accept responsibility for poor or mediocre performance based solely on the, "oh it's my fault" default, we carry. With this one we should get scientific; we should review analytically. We should detach emotionally and remember that although we are talking about connection and that's important, a lot of what we are about to cover are little bits of website code. 1's and 0's over and over. What we will see here should inform us, not berate us… nor, which is often the case, validate us. Let's stick a pin in that, we aren't quite ready for THAT conversation just yet.

It's really important for me to state that the information I share here will outdate a little as time goes on and my team will probably have to remind me to re-write this particular chapter for new editions in the future. Much like human behaviour, the data thereof changes and so it should!

Inevitably this chapter may start to sway your opinion in which platforms you choose to spend your content time in. If you are considering your options with this side of your business, I would love for you to have an open mind, try not to remember the blocks that we spoke about in the other chapters. If you're the type of person who's like, "Oh, I really hate Facebook." Just do me a favour and take off that hate for Facebook, or "I hate YouTube" or "I hate Tiktok" or whichever you have previously rejected. Just stick it down somewhere for me, just for today, and keep an open mind and let me give you some information that may or may not be new to you. Then you can make an educated decision in where you want to push your own focus. Okay? Okay!

At the point of writing this chapter, more than half of the world now uses social media. So that's 59% of the entire population. I know that probably seems like a no brainer because, duh, Dawn, it's not breaking news that people are online. But when you actually think about how many people that is, it's a real lot. Its more people than you can probably, comfortably, imagine in your mind's eye.

4.8 billion people around the world now use social media with 150 million new users that have come online just within the last 12 months (2023). So, it's only going to get bigger and bigger and bigger. Every single year, we think social media has peaked, this is the time we plateau and the numbers will stop rising. We are always wrong. Some cultures around the world have not embraced it yet and it is going to continue in growth for some time.

Now understand, this isn't small growth either, even though the numbers are high, we haven't even got to 80% or to 90% of the population yet. At the time of writing this, it's still kind of at the halfway point and if you are not catching my drift let me say it again, **It's a lot of people, but it hasn't yet fully peaked.**

The average monthly time spent using social media is twenty hours globally per person, and that is an average, because we all know people who check their socials more than they change their clothes, and we all have people in our lives who either don't get it, or are too old, to be emotionally attached to the inevitable dopamine hit you get with each increasing "like".

If you break that twenty hours down however it is still quite a significant amount of time, every single day, especially if you think about someone like Fred, who perhaps works on a building site. He is on it before work, at his lunch break and likely sneakily in between too, then in the evenings. Our mobile phone culture has us glued to the screens and social media is the top spot for where people spend their time!

If you think about that, it might just be five minutes here, it might be three minutes there.

But it mounts up right?! What's more, from a business advertising point of view, you are sat in Fred's van with him. You're sat on his sofa at night. Let's face it, Fred is taking you with him to the toilet each day, (don't think too much about that last one). The possibilities for getting in front of your desired audiences are, well, pretty boundless. Maybe there's some algorithm to arm wrestle but you yourself, have probably put more blocks on your visibility than the algorithm ever could.

And we've got 4.8 billion total social media users across all platforms. What that actually means is, we have more people using more platforms than just one.

Typically, this works out that the average person bounces between seven different social networks per month. Sheesh - that is a lot of places to go for your social digital entertainment.

General advice through Google and suchlike will tell you that you need to be on all these Seven or more platforms. But I would love, love, love to invite you to have a look at the platforms out there, figure out what their features and benefits are for you, and choose ones you will enjoy being on and creating content for.

Then and only then can you decide where you're going to focus your attention and your precious, precious time. Hear me when I say you do not need to be on all of those seven different social media platforms in order to have a successful business and grow an audience. In fact, trying to spread yourself too thinly over multiple platforms within the first five years of your business can have more of a negative effect rather than a positive one.

You also do not have to reject all but one either. There are smart ways for you to build with focus and fold more visibility practises in as you grow and as your business resources allow for a higher marketing budget.

You need to know who you want to see you, and you need to know that some of your ideal clients are on any of these platforms. When it comes to choosing which ones to focus on, you can only try and learn but no matter what, there is no such thing as WRONG.

Just a little information about Tiktok because I get asked all the time if it is really necessary to be added to this players list.

Tiktok is the fastest growing social media network with a staggering 180% user growth rate in the US in the past two years, with the TikTok app being downloaded 3 billion times. Now, there's a bit of a disclaimer here for those of us that follow the news when it comes to social media as part of our job. There was a massive court case going on in America, where they were considering setting a precedent over social media and they used TikTok as the example. You *could say* scapegoat, but that perhaps could be seen as a political opinion so we will say, ahem, their example.

So, some of the "important people" in the US have decided that Tiktok is bad, social media is bad, (why can I hear "drugs are bad, McKay?" from Mr. Mackey's character from South Park in my head when I type this) and in their eyes Tiktok needs to be banned.

There's no way to know whether they will pass this law one day, if they will keep going or what will happen in the future with the people who feel this way.

If I had written this book, five or six, years ago, I would have snapped here and said there's no way, in any dimension, that the US will ban an app that supports over 5 million of its businesses and then so much of its economic power. But after Trump being president and the Roe Vs Wade debacle I cannot in good faith tell you anything about America and therefore won't bore you with an opinion.

There is an awful lot going on and much of it difficult for the standard compassionate human to understand. If they do ever ban Tiktok, it's going to be really, really bad for US businesses. Yes, it could potentially spill over into the UK and the rest of the western world because *you could say* that for some reason, we all like to adopt what America does. I am sure some people *may believe* it has something to do with their "powerful people" having our "powerful peoples" balls in a Jar or something?

This book is not intended to be political *at all,* but you *could be* of an opinion, that because Tiktok has not (at the time of writing this book) had any funding, censorship nor political influence added to it, it may not be the most popular to those who seek to have narrative sway in the media. You *could* perhaps entertain the conclusion that the reason there is a rise in fake information on the platform, is because it is being used as a freedom of information platform due to this fact.

Lots of information (both good and bad) is being shared between humans who are having their media guided by certain narratives on other platforms and in mainstream media. You *could say* such a powerful connective tool that is independent and not regulated by any particular body or government power could potentially be worrying for those who seek to withhold, gatekeep or sway public information.

Of course, I am not saying anything, I am batting my eyelashes, sipping my coffee, and simply sharing that which *could be said.*

So, who are the main players? Let's look at Facebook.

Facebook

First, who isn't on Facebook? Especially after the covid years. Meta, as it is now known, owns Facebook, and coincidentally also Instagram. But Facebook specifically has a number of monthly active users of 3.3 billion. The most exciting thing about Facebook is it is now the third most visited site and is only beaten by YouTube and Google. And YouTube if you didn't know is owned by Google. So that's the reason why YouTube gets a higher ranking on searches because it's owned by the search. It's not what you know....

So, to be the third most visited site and not owned by Google, and who isn't influenced by the search giants own agenda, actually makes it pretty much like a clean number one, if you think about it. And 81.8% of users only look at Facebook on a mobile phone EVER. So, whenever you're considering a sales page, a post, or a cover photo for your groups etc, remember that optimising it for mobile is always going to be more important than optimising it on a computer.

The people who do look at Facebook on a computer are businesspeople who are also using Facebook for business reasons, myself included, we look on laptops,PC's, giant monitors and so forth. What is interesting is we tend to have the computer in front of us, and we'll also have our phones right under our noses. We will be in the same platform and be looking at it through three different screens. Most people however only do it on their phone.

Over 500 million people watch Facebook stories. Even though Facebook stories wasn't a thing a few years ago, it is now here to stay. The gift that came from Snapchat, that then got moved on to Instagram, before also landing on Facebook. There is a massive increase of people watching Facebook stories. So, if you aren't utilising stories on Facebook, you might want to consider adding that into your strategy. 1.8 billion use Facebook groups every single month too. If you're sat there thinking I'm so done and bored with the idea of Facebook groups, it's been done and It's dead as a dodo now. It really isn't.

We've got a ridiculously large amount of people who not only enjoy using Facebook groups, but almost exclusively use Facebook just for the groups.

I know that sometimes when you're posting and you're feeling like nobody is interacting, and nobody's reading, and nobody's watching, nobody's commenting, you're thinking, "is there really any point in posting or putting myself out there or trying to be visible?"
You read these statistics of how many users there are, and that they are all spending hours and hours every month on the platforms too. Why aren't they interacting, what am I doing wrong?

I want you to remember this next tasty bite of information: the average user only likes **10** posts, only makes **four** comments, and perhaps clicks on **eight** ads **monthly**, despite people being on there for at least two and a half hours a day. Think about that. In terms of actual time, they HARDLY EVER INTERACT.

This might be quite a mic drop moment so I am going to give you a minute to process that.

Feel free to step away from the book if you need to. The whole "It's not you, it's them"
of it is quite important for me to express, as it is not what your standard marketing guru would openly share. It should fuel your motivation in what I like to call the "invisible metric" which is those who see you and subliminally take you in, but, do not show on your data points for quite some time.

I personally can comment on 10 posts, like 100 posts and click on 25 adverts, especially if Chanel or Dior come up on my Facebook all within about 10 minutes. But your average user, the people we're often trying to connect with my darlings don't actually interact on the socials very often at all. They are too busy consuming, and often not realising they aren't interacting. So when you're there, and it's like Tumbleweed city and you think no one's listening, no one's watching, no one's going to see you. Please know, they are.

There is a secret hidden metric that isn't been shown to you; the lurker, the reader, the secret watcher.

Interestingly 72.6% of Facebook users also frequently use YouTube, so there is a correlation between people who like Facebook. They also like YouTube, and WhatsApp. Remember that we said that humans like to skip over approximately seven social media lily pads each month, it won't shock you then, that Facebook users also like Instagram!!

Many a savvy marketer may refer to these platforms as the top four, these are your main players. 50% of business-to-business decision makers will use Facebook for research. If you're looking for a course, or you're looking to work with somebody, you're looking to hire somebody as a VA, or you're looking for somebody to come and teach your team how to paint or whatever, you might go on Facebook 50% of the time and use it as a research tool alone. That makes it the top traditional social network for b2b research, with only YouTube coming in close at 46%.

Don't overlook Facebook when marketing to a business audience. Facebook would always be my initial suggestion to use. Searches for local businesses have also seen increases up to 52%.

We talk a lot about engagement rates but the average

engagement rate for Facebook posts is 0.12%. So if you're looking at your insights, and you're looking at your engagement rate, and you're thinking, "Oh this is ridiculous, my engagement rate is only 3%." You're already winning, you just don't think you are. Often when we are comparing notes, we are doing so with peers, and idols, that have full marketing teams and people like, well me, behind them creating killer strategy and executing it in real time.

For the rest of the entrepreneurial world who are not in marketing, it's good to recognise where you are in a good way. You could be in the top 20% of all content and not even realise how well you are doing!

Facebook Live still had 2 billion viewers in 2023. Some of the general advice people, out there in digital business land, have been saying that video doesn't work on Facebook anymore and that video only works on Tiktok and on YouTube, but they are sadly mistaken. Facebook Live is still working. Having 2 billion viewers and a conversion rate of 2% is still some good cheddar. You know what BBC would do with 2 billion viewers? They'd keep that show running!

When you're making the decision between recording a static video and going live, think about the fact that Facebook users watch live videos for three times longer than a regular video. If that video is static, the psychology there is that they can come back to it, and they don't have to interact with you to do so. They think they will, but in reality, they often won't. A static video has no urgency. Nor does it have any real time connectivity. If your watchers have got the opportunity to chat to you in the comments, or to see you live, they will watch it for much longer and are more likely to get involved and interact.

Static videos do still have a place though, so if you love a prerecord situation, do not despair. There are effective ways to use both, you just need to match the right style of media to the right message.

Within Facebook you have lots of different areas where you can show up. You have your personal profile, which you do have the opportunity to turn into a professional public figure profile or creator type profile. You have business pages, groups, chats, DM's, stories rooms (which is just like chats).

These spaces give you the opportunity to directly connect to your audience for free!

One thing you should know is that Meta wants to take over the world. The functionality that is available now is amazing, but it is never going to stop growing!

You also have direct messages and direct messages are a powerful tool for personal outreach. They give you the opportunity to directly connect to your audience, and this is brilliant when you're attracting people to buy from you.

I think everybody will agree that Facebook warrants a bit of our focus in terms of growing an audience and can help us to earn some money in our businesses. It's quite obvious from the statistics.

Let's do a speed round of some of the others too.

Instagram

Your monthly active users is 1.3 billion on the platform

for twenty-nine minutes. Average daily uses are very similar to Facebook's 81%, users use Instagram to research products too. You've got 70% of all Instagram users watching stories daily. That might make you think, "Okay, so stories on Instagram, they're not old, they're still huge."

50% of users are visiting websites from Instagram after seeing a product or a service on that platform, which means that if you're ever wanting to drive traffic to a product, service, or an area of your website, Instagram can be very useful.

0.54% is the average engagement rate for business accounts on Instagram. So you'll notice that the engagement rate on Instagram is much, much higher than Facebook. This platform is beginning to lose its trendy status but is still performing as a relationship building platform. It is really, really good per connection. When using Instagram, you may find it's easier to gain a lot of love from the right ideal clients.

200 million Instagram users visit at least one business profile daily. Within Instagram, you have one profile per login. There are now lots of features that are similar to Facebook because they're owned by the same people.

YouTube

YouTube has 2.1 billion active users. And on average the users spend 59 minutes on YouTube every day. So that's an hour, which, in "OMG I need to get their attention in 3 seconds" social media land, translates to a ridiculously long amount of time. YouTube is one of the rare places where we're still getting long form content. 50.9% of business-to-business decision makers are using YouTube to research purchases, making it the most use social media platform for advertising for this purpose.

Now, have you ever watched a video on YouTube and the maker of the video has said "Hey, this video is sponsored by honey savings and discount," "this video is sponsored by sleep well." "This video is sponsored by wowcher"?

That's because they know that people who are watching YouTube are weapons of massive consumption, aka consumers, they're b2b decision makers and they are your standard friends who are looking for the next "DeWalt battery packed on site radio" to drop. Know that people check YouTube when they want to work with you, but they're also using it as a very, very high product-based research centre and most importantly for ENTERTAINMENT.

YouTube ads are so popular with such a high return on investment because they are to us what tv commercials used to be before Netflix.

The good thing about YouTube, when you use it for connection-based content, is that it's forcing you to use video, and somebody can see your body language and your face and hear your voice. The platform organically promotes the know, like and trust factor, all good personal brands and small businesses are looking to tap into. You are going to fall in like with somebody, trust them, understand them, and want to work with them faster when you can see who they really are.

As animals (which we still kinda are) we are looking to evaluate, and when you can see that they're not faking it, when you can see them regularly, when they show up and there is consistency, you will emotionally attach - even if on a shallow level. Everything your future consumers are looking for, can be found on video. This is the one that really excites me, because people think, "oh, yeah, YouTube only has one screen/district."

YouTube has one screen, right? It's just the one screen where you search for videos. Wrong. Wrong, wrong, wrong.

YouTube has playlists, like Spotify, like Amazon music. You can create a playlist of all your specific videos and send one link to your clients so that they can watch that entire playlist from that one link.

You can create videos that are in a series that have real episodes. And not only can you create them and put them out on YouTube, they don't have to be scattered around. You can organise them so that they can be watched in a specific order. In terms of messaging, in terms of delivery, that's really good. And it's something that is super exciting.

Because you can't do that with podcasts, you put your podcast out every single week, it usually goes out at the same time of the week, and it's just, kind of a medley. But at YouTube, you can organise everything. So if you've got more than one ideal client, this can be super helpful. Like this is the playlist for my corporate clients. This is the playlist for my positive psychology clients. This is the playlist for my small business owners. This is the playlist for my salon owners, whatever you want, you can create.

One of the sexy things about YouTube and one of the

things that I love about YouTube is that they do not restrict links in the description. For instance, when I was doing the Audience Attraction live launch for my signature course, I was putting in my interviews with my previous alumni about how wonderful this course is on YouTube. And then I was putting the sales page link in the description. So if you're watching this video, and you're thinking, "Man, this is for me, I really want to work with Dawni on structure, this is going to change my life, I'm going to buy this course," you need not look any further. The link to buy it is right there. It's like casually listing a product.

You could consider every free video you add to Youtube like a lead generating funnel and a casual sales post, on a search engine that already has billions of users. It's great. It's fantastic for business. You also have a good comments section on YouTube. People do comment on YouTube videos, believe you me, they will let you know how things are going, if they like that video, if they want more of that video. And you can interact with people and engage with people the same way as you would on any other programme. They also have stories and people are watching YouTube stories.

They're called YouTube shorts but would a "rose smell as sweet with a different name"? and they are videos, but they are quick, short, snappy videos a bit like Tiktok a bit like Reels, but YouTube's version of them, and you can put them up daily.

You also have a little area in YouTube called communities, which is their version of groups, basically, where you can chat to other people who are watching the video at the same time. Do you remember watch parties on Facebook, they no longer exist, but you could watch a video with lots of other people and chat to each other at the same time. It was like a shared experience. That's what communities are on YouTube. You also have discovery, obviously, your standard news feed, which everybody knows, but what's good about YouTube is that once you get to a certain level of views, you can earn so much passive income aka dollar aka cheddar aka money.

As business owners we use it for visibility and to promote ourselves. But also, some people use YouTube just **as their business**, they make videos on YouTube of things like ASMR or helpful tips for cleaning and it is their entire business. They aren't relying on a product or merchandise, they are paid purely for exposure, and views. So there is a double factored opportunity for you to increase your income through this platform.

LinkedIn

LinkedIn has 875 million members. It's not as big as the others, but it is growing. It used to have a bit of a stuffy reputation for its business specific theme. The idea around LinkedIn is it's your corporate clients professional hang out, traditional professional interactions and your networking type of connections.

42% of users are female, that number is growing every single year. But we still have more dudes on LinkedIn than we have women. You *could say* it's the corporate patriarchy due to there being a discrepancy in how many women there are in managerial roles and those which would use networking as a power.

Interestingly 60% of LinkedIn users are between 25 and

34 years old, you see a trend here, Facebook, Instagram, and LinkedIn, 25 and 34. It's the sweet spot. But do not think that your niche, your ideal client isn't on there, it's just that it's a high percentage. It doesn't mean that there isn't a lovely sized percentage of yours as well.

Despite its reputation, it is getting warmer over there, less stuffy and a place where you can enjoy consuming content and not just those for your HR department. 52 million people use LinkedIn to search for jobs each week. So if you're hiring, or if you're looking to work with people, or if you're looking to connect with people to collaborate, LinkedIn is a powerful tool. If you ever want to get in the corporate gig, LinkedIn might be for you.

One thing to know for the average online business owner, people will check you out on LinkedIn before doing corporate gigs with you. They will check you out before applying for a job with you. They may even check you out before offering to have you as a guest on their podcast. Personal posts are getting much more traction on LinkedIn and now are really starting to perform.

One of the beautiful things about it, is it gives you a history when you look at someone's profile, so when I say I have worked with the world's biggest brands in the Luxury retail market, you can go and see if I actually have, or if I am talking balderdash.

You have your profile over there; you can also have an organisation page very similar to Facebook, but you can't create jobs. You also can have stories on LinkedIn, you can have groups and communities too. But one of the things I really love about LinkedIn is the articles. Blogging and articles over on LinkedIn is incredibly powerful. Just this one feature can be good for bringing in audiences/leads and clients.

If you're the type of person who makes a blog for your website anyway, it might not hurt to repurpose that on your LinkedIn profile, because it's already made. You can get two great pieces of content for the price of one, out of your energy output.

LinkedIn is a networking place. The idea on LinkedIn is to be a bit of a business hussy, I give you full permission to connect around on LinkedIn and connect with as many people as humanly possible.

Twitter

I've got a lot to say about Twitter, but I'm gonna run through it rather fast because we are sharing straight up facts and swerving my own personal opinions today.

450 million active users over on Twitter, 20.7% are in the age demographic of 35 to 49 years old, to a slightly older age bracket. People understood Twitter before they understood anything else. Mainly because it was primarily text and one of the first socials to allow for the "everyone's a critic" psychology of sharing your thoughts in short form regularly.

Four hours and forty minutes is the average monthly time spent on Twitter, which again, as you can see across the platforms is pretty solid, but one that we wouldn't consider to be a main player in 2023. 2% of business to businesses use Twitter as a marketing tool.

Twitter is the place where you will find the biggest companies, political rounds, perfect for political rants as well. With half a billion tweets sent out a day, 40% of Twitter users reported buying something.

The overall vibe of buying behaviours is that people aren't going to Twitter to buy things. People are going to Twitter to read comedy tweets. To see whether Aldi and Marks and Spencer, have another very public beef or to find out what the bloody hell Elon Musk is doing now, or Kanye for that matter.

They are going to look at the political stuff, to tell their political leaders that there are no beds in the local hospital, or to complain that they're in a queue because the item that they ordered didn't arrive on time. People are using twitter as a news forum.

Snapchat

Who uses Snapchat? You've got your bird's eye view, if you're going for the 16-year-olds, tablet babies and GEN Z, I hate to say this, but it's just the truth - you need snapchat.

Snapchat is where you want to be. I don't know what else to say. The cool kids are on it. And that's, that's basically how it is. You can sniff at its validity but then you can't sniff at the 375 million kids on it, who are influencing what their parents buy them, or what they buy themselves from their ridiculous YouTube ad earnings from those Roblox walkthrough videos they post!

It's powerful, don't overlook it. Big Brands love it, it's really good for them to pre nurture even younger audiences too, with 1 million users aged 18 to 24. You'll also find more underage users on Snapchat, and Tiktok than anywhere else on the internet. Toy companies have been directly marketing to kids and meeting them on their level for decades.

Pre nurture of an audience that isn't yet your main demographic is a practise that is here to stay. Snapchat and Tiktok are the ones that are having to kick, 8,9,10 ,11-year-old kids off because they're not of age or add parental features as well.

They're the ones that are struggling to keep the right safety boundaries in place. But they're also the ones that are super fun with the filters and are playing to that younger, playful demographic. So, it makes total sense, right? That's where the kids are trying to hang out.

5+ billion snaps are sent out daily, quite a lot. Those are what they call the disappear bubble snaps, which means that you can send somebody a picture and five seconds later that picture disappears. It's like being in real time, but it's not in real time.

There is also big business for people who work in augmenting reality and avatars over there. Creatives such as photograph editors, photography, video, videographers can embrace the fun, flirtatious and creative styles that filtering must offer. It can be a really big business, using filters, creating filters, teaching people how to use filters, all that good stuff.

On Snapchat the camera is its most popular feature and is opened 20 times a day, with half its users actively using the Discovery Centre as well. So people are also looking to connect with other people on there.

Tiktok continued

As we have already discussed, Tiktok is ridiculously large, active users equals 1.3 billion users as of 2023 remember. It's downloaded over 3 billion times. About 80 million active users in the US, an average of 75 minutes per day. So, here's the thing. Out of all the platforms that I've spoken about, where are people staying the longest?

YouTube and Tiktok?

There's a reason for that, my darlings....it's because people want video. Don't hate me, I'm going to support you through this. I know it's hard. Okay?!

But I must tell you how it is, so that we can work out your bespoke strategy, that works for you, but also that works for the business. They want video, guys. Okay?! All the data points towards that. And it's because our audiences get to know us on video, it's because they feel like they're with us on video. It's because we are just primates trying to connect to each other. And even though we're doing it through digital screens and fancy microphones, we just want to connect with some other people of our species. There's a real deep primary reason for why that is the way it is.

Let's look at some of the other ones that aren't social media. **Pinterest,** Pinterest is bloody wonderful for visibility, but you're not putting videos on Pinterest. This is an information and inspiration hold area. It's not social, which just means It's not meant for immediate interaction in real time. It doesn't mean it isn't valuable. It is a great visibility platform, although you may nurture your audience on socials, your social doesn't have to be the only place we get the audience from.

450 million monthly active users. That's huge. If your ideal client is a woman, or identifies as a woman, you're going to go for 76.2% of the women that are using Pinterest. It is targeted towards feminine energy, Gen Z users are up 40% year on year, so the younger population are coming on board. It's not just for people of a certain age demographic. The young ones are using it too. They're using it for their university assessments, and even high schoolers are using it towards their GCSE revision. It's an information sharing base. And it's heavily involved with Google.

I would say it is in a committed situationship with Google. Opportunities to be found by people who don't know you exist. People are using it to inspire purchases, they are making pinboards and adding what they want to buy, what they're saving up for, what they're interested in. It is a brilliant place for people to research and to be found. It's not a great place for a lead magnet, opt in or blog.

It is THE place. People use Pinterest search like Google, which is massive. Remember, we want to be searchable, we want to be found.

Now I've covered a lot of ground there and would love for you to have a little think about which one/s you are swaying towards.

You've got time to consider. Maybe fold this page over. Go grab yourself a highlighter and butcher the margin with your thoughts. But think about which one is going to be your top priority and then make a plan to work on that one first. Remember this birds eye view is intended to inform and delight, not overwhelm. At the end of the day these are all just different screens where we share different things to make the most of connecting to each other.

CHAPTER FOUR
- THE INSIDE /
OUTSIDE VISIBILITY

If you haven't been in digital marketing as an arena before, you may never have heard the fancy Jargon associated. Trust me when I say there are many fancy words to describe the customer journey and how to nurture leads and audiences into fully paying, fully grateful super fan clients. When explaining the Inside vs Outside method, I have had social media managers in training with tears in their eyes. People who have been in digital marketing for decades, patting me on the back and thanking me. People come away from this concept, renewed with a different perspective and it is down to one thing.

Simplicity.

This chapter allows you to place audiences in your little mind maps, and that can be really really helpful. Once you have an idea of how it works, it can act as a reminder. Especially when you're doing your content, planning how to create and lift different departments within your content, and in the way that you speak to people wherever they are at in your journey.

The inside outside visibility is all about you figuring out what part of your content and messaging is your outer representative, the brand representative, the brand awareness, the attraction, and what part of your content is the inner visibility and nurture for your more qualified and warm audience members!

When you show up online for the first time, you are usually doing so to begin an inside visibility. If you are using your personal profile, you are probably showing up to friends, family, ex colleagues and that nice lady who lives next door but one.

You think you stole the mic from Dave Grohl and stormed the stage at Glastonbury but in reality, you whispered something over dinner.

It is easy to forget what is public and what is reserved for different groups of people, based on your settings.

By the time you have audiences who are on your email lists and hanging out in your Facebook groups, you may have realised that one piece of content does not serve all the rooms you are in. Serving your audience according to environment, is **ROCKSTAR MARKETING**, and what's best about that also is that it is free to do, mainly.

You will have people who are following you, some who are in your DMs. They are in 2 different rooms.

So if you've ever been to an event like Social Media Marketing World, you'll go into the main arena, and the main arena will be full of people, people who've bought a ticket to be there, and then there'll be different rooms. There will be workshops, and you can go into the different specific rooms, and in those rooms, you will be more specific about whatever the subject is.

Your customer journey is the same. Someone who follows you on Instagram for a day, may not understand something that you reference, the same way that someone who has been in your groups and on your email list for 4 years would.

You begin to be multi-faceted in the way you show up for your people, allowing for each part to be served in the best way for them.

Your brand representation and brand awareness is your first meet. It could be considered your shop window. This is your open, public, and free for all representative. This is your *OUTSIDE VISIBILITY*

This is your PR, your Google business. This is your website. If your settings are public; Instagram, LinkedIn, Pinterest, articles you wrote, YouTube channel videos, podcasts etc etc. They're all your OUTSIDE VISIBILITY

There are many different areas that you've got, that are outside visibility.

Okay, what are the other areas that are outside visibility?

Open information for all, but not specifically advertising.

It is an opportunity for people to be intrigued enough to want to join your email list or hop on into your free group. It is your normal and general open forum of business self-expression and connection.

The aim for these spaces may seem complex when you are considering your content strategy. I could tell you that you need to cross populate your messaging and use psychology to present ideas in a way that would stop the scroll. All of these are exceptional tools, often not immediately necessary.

Your outside spaces serve on thing only, getting audience members through the customer journey and into your inside spaces. People often don't just join another group or sign up to another freebie the way they did in 2018. Now there needs to be a bit more of a draw to it.

You want people to know that if they don't come into your inside spaces, like your email list, or your Facebook groups, or any of these things that are more insular, that they will miss out on key content, community, and opportunity.

You are offering up additional benefits to being inside environments you have a little more control over. You are saying "There are things that you can get by being a loyal follower to me, that you won't get if you're just a general public follower."

This is a technique for social media specifically, it works really, really well on all the social media platforms. It offers the opportunity to give sneak peeks or cliffhangers or titbits of information. So for instance, you might put something out that is public, and you might say "I'm going to do a free masterclass on drop shipping." "In order to watch the free masterclass on drop shipping, you need to sign up to my email list," or "you need to join my free group." Any of those and other types of things can be used to give the link.

It creates intrigue, which is different from advertising. It is an invite for something of value. It's a completely different vibe. Intrigue is where you get somebody interested and curious about what it is that you can do to support them.

What I love about this, is that it allows you to share information but without being overly salesy.

I like to call my groups "Safe houses," because for me, I really love that I can control the environment.

Got a grumpy Gertie? - not anymore, she's been booted.

Want to spread some joy with affirmations and positive statements?

Great! – no-one can stop you!

You. Get. To. Decide... when you are using areas on the internet where you have full control over the environment.

In outside visibility, you can't control the entire environment. You must relinquish control. But on inside spaces, you control most of it.

For instance, in my Facebook group, if I decide that you can't promote yourself, and then you promote yourself in my group, I boot you. Simple! I create the ecosystem in that Facebook group for everyone's comfort, including my own. I can't necessarily stop Shayla from advertising herself on her own profile on Facebook, right? that's not something that's in my control but inside my group, it is.

It's the difference between the perspectives of where we are in those different areas.

Any space that could be considered public is an outside one. What we are aiming to do is make it desirable for someone to join an inner circle of some type.

Psychologically, this is a positive for everyone involved. The audience member feels inclusion and is welcomed into a community of sorts. You can give a focus that is far harder to measure when not within a controlled area.

When sharing content on the outside, our main goal is to get to a point where the person interacts and wants to be part of your world in a deeper way. This is effectively the only step we need. Some people will meet you online in the outside visibility, click a button, and buy from you, moving all the way round the board and passing Go before you have even had chance to catch their name, - but it is rare.

Most of your sales activations will come from your inner circles, your inward spaces, safe houses, chats, groups, and email lists and that is really where we want our audience to be.

You can view your Facebook profile as a non-brand and see what it shows on your timeline.

More passive outside visibility's you may not have thought of, are your personal bio's. The little part that you have on all your social medias that help people to get to know you. Any freebies, that you have on your website. Email footers and Casual affiliates.

When I say casual affiliates, what I mean by this is, you may not realise it, but as you have been able to connect to other people in your networks, you will already have people who are on your side and interested in referring you to others naturally. I mean people we've not asked to refer us, people we're NOT paying to give us referrals. Those amazing humans that do it out of the goodness of their heart and build connections to be helpful to two people at the same time.

Don't disregard the power or neglect how powerful and passive this behaviour from your audience can be.

You're not the one that's asking for the sale, and the immediate social proof is evident! It is pure gold, and something to be grateful for. Once it is out there, you could still be gaining new leads six months, twelve months, two years, four years, six years, later and later, with these amazing audience members still naturally bringing great people into your network. Blooming marvellous!

If you compare casual affiliates and referrals to a post on Instagram and see how much longevity it has, you will find it easy to see that it has a very short shelf life. Posted six years ago would likely mean that no one has looked at it for five years and around 360 days.

Nurture the people first!

Advertise yourself second!

That doesn't mean don't post, it means remember the

power of what you're posting and ripple effect associated. "Buy my stuff" will only ever get you so far.

When we bring the attention to spaces that are more exclusive and yet welcoming to most, if not all, we are inviting our audience to go a little deeper in interaction and engagement. Being invited to the party is not something to be sniffed at. It is a powerful way to let your audience know that they are valued, and to give them opportunities to engage with you in a more direct manner, but under the right boundaries and circumstances.

Nurture is like growing tomatoes. You need the right conditions, you must take very good care of them, tend to them, and ensure that you don't neglect them. It is a long-haul situation, a marathon not a sprint. It might take somebody five months; it might take somebody five years to find themselves harmoniously in the 3% bracket of your audience who wants to buy.

A basic customer journey would look like this.

> find them.
> entice/ invite them in, remember to explain what they are missing by only consuming your public content, versus what they'd get in your communities / Facebook groups and your email lists.
> Offer loyalty rewards *(for me this is my free group getting the opportunity to buy our best deals before anyone else - a bit like a waitlist for all presales, my pretties get first refusal.) Hence why we hardly ever get to go public with our offers. We tend to sell out fast.*
> Nurture and connect.
> LISTEN (There's a full chapter in the book about this)

> Offer and invite *(sell)*

AND repeat over and over until the new stream of leads starts to naturally grow from your amazing public visibility and exceptional emotive content!

Loyalty rewarding and nurture are powerful but you can't expect your audience to invest in you if you do not invest in them too. You should take the time to get to know things about them. I am not expecting you to know by name and phone number thousands of people. You're not Erin Brockovich. But there is merit in taking the time to fully give your audience your attention and whenever possible to respond to them.

Reply to comments and DMs as often as humanly possible. Let them know that even in your busy world they matter. Relate to them.

One of the easiest ways to relate is to jump into their shoes, like Mary Poppins jumping into the chalk drawing, and see what it feels like to embody their situation.

Exercise : Ask yourself these questions

Why should they be interested in you?

How do you fit into their world?

What positives do you bring them? (this is a big one).

What calls to action do you want from them, what do you want them to do?

How can you make it super easy for them?

How can you make it just one click?

Think about it.

What qualifies them?
What are you looking for in an ideal client?

Are you looking for smart?
Are you looking for kind?
Are you looking for warmth?
Are you looking for vulnerable?
Are you looking for open?
Are you looking for honest?

What.. qualifies... them?

If you want to know if somebody's it, write a post about kindness, see how many people respond to it?

Don't be scared to be a little controversial if it aligns with your values truthfully.

I once "de-qualified" and cleared out a massive chunk of my email list with one email titled, "Thank God Trump no longer has the Nuke codes."

It took 24 hours for nearly all Trump supporters to remove themselves from my list, a lot of them reporting me for spam, - unsurprising behaviour.

It shouldn't worry you when things like that happen. Polarising content will show you those who have similar beliefs, values, and ethics and those who do not.

If you lose people that is okay! They could not get too close to the bullseye, which is your dreamy clients then. Don't be scared. Do I feel bad that Trump supporters left my list? -no! Does their political support of a cheesy

Wotsit make them bad people?- no!! They just aren't MY people! And that's okay!

You want to weed out anyone who may not be on your wavelength before you welcome them into a group or community setting, because it only takes a couple of counter personalities to change the whole vibe in a group setting, and the energy of those spaces and places is everything!

Boot! remove! block! and protect those spaces above all else!

Remember that emails, although ultra-modern, are our versions of letters. And letters to each other, whether left in a bottle or sent by carrier pigeon, were, and still should be, rather personal.

When you are writing to your ideal client, write directly to that one person and don't be afraid to share real life and personal stories.

If you're on my email list, you will know that my emails are peppered with personal stories. I tell you about my life. I tell you about my mum getting dragged into hospital, I tell you about the time that I crashed into Freddie Mercury's car *(not the actual Freddie Mercury but a professional tribute).*

In those love letters from me to you, I tell you about my family, my husband, my kids, my dad, my funny stories. In those areas you will learn that I was once in a band called "thermal sock," and that I have a deep hatred for the band ABBA. Can't believe I gave them a mention in my book!

When it comes to your loyal audience feeling secure in those extra special community spaces, you need to keep considering why they should maintain their interest in you?

It's not about you or me!

You're sharing to let someone in, to let them get to know you.

Think about:

How do you fit into their world now that they are on your email list?
Or in your group?
How much more do they get from you?
How much more do they get for their loyalty?
Can you invite them to work with you?
Can you offer things for them to come and work with you?
How can you encourage them to engage, not just with you, but also with the community?
How can you encourage them to get in with your people?

Every single new person that comes into your free group is a part of the puzzle that makes the collective a beautiful picture. They get to walk into a space where the members interactions and engagements are cultivated for good, for people to thrive and support.

That, in itself, is pretty priceless!

When someone arrives to the space who has related to you, it would be pretty difficult for them not to fall in. We fall in line with the energy and the vibe due to the environment and the eco system within.

Engaging with other people, not just the host, becomes easy because a new member will recognise that the space is filled with people just like them, who share similar views on the world.

What you know is lovely but who you know is most valuable. Get to know them and let them know you.

In your group think about:

How can you add value to their day?

And how can you continue to place yourself as the expert every day?

How can you let people know? (don't forget, I've got this sauce, and I can help you).

What can you offer for free to your people and how do you go about rewarding loyalty?

There is also another level to this:

Your paid spaces! Memberships, courses, subscriptions, (if you have them) and if you do, I invite you to think about these questions of strategic value:

How can you treat them like the valued client that they are?
How can you make them realise how grateful you are?
To what degree of your focus, love, and attention will they get by being a paid client?

Because they've gotten to the highest tier of your visibility!

How can you maintain their interest in you?
How do you fit into their world Now?

What additional positives do you bring to them by working with them in this way?
And what did they get for their loyalty?

Okay.

How can you elevate them?
How can you support their goals?
How can you maintain a quality relationship with them?
And how can you support their needs and wants even better?
How can you support their goals outside of the service that they paid for?

Can you offer them more and support them further than the service they paid for? Don't use this as permission from me to abandon your boundaries! Definitely not! But how can you ensure they know that you value them more than currency? If you don't value them more than currency, or you're reading this and thinking it is a bunch of over emotional tripe - then stop reading here and throw this book out of the closest window, because it is not for you!

Wooing your audience is a thing. Let's just lay that out there. You wouldn't go up to your first date and upon introducing yourself, forcefully suggest you get physical. *I am trying so hard not to have naughty entendres in this paragraph and yet am painfully aware of "Lay" and "hard" …Ooops!*

Business relationships share a refinement that you would see in Bridgerton style polite dating. Tim Curry said it best when he slowly muttered **Annn**….**tici…iii** ………… **pation**! before riding his steel lift to another floor. *"Riding,"* oh dear!

What I am trying to say, in a less only fans kind of way, is that you can't go straight for the kill. You need to warm your audience up to you and your community and your world before you expect them to buy from you.

Trying it on too early and not asking consent will get you into trouble as a sales perv!

So don't do that! Allow relationships to naturally bloom, for friendships to grow and for there to be the sweet, sweet environment that is completely devoid of expectation.

There should be as many experiences of expectation and entitlement from the host as my mum has boobs. That number is ZERO. Remove them like the surgeon did with my mother and throw them in the incinerator never to return.

Entitlement - Expectation and Desperation will murder your opportunity to sell, but they will also poison your genuine relationships and stop others from blooming too.

On your outside visibility remember to invite them in to your exclusive and "inward visibility hubs." Once inside, you treat them like the valued guests they are, and make sure they are comfortable.

It is simple if you strip it back.

You noticed "strip" didn't you? - isn't psychology great.

CHAPTER FIVE - DREAMY CLIENTS AND WHERE TO FIND THEM.

When it comes to finding dreamy clients, the methods can become a bit of an enigma. They're the holy grail of marketing, everyone has an opinion about them, but most feel like they've never really seen enough of them, to be fully sure.

First of all, what even is a **dreamy** client?

Well, a dreamy client is the type of client who recognises your talents, they are the ones who are excited to work with you. They are the ones that don't have to be convinced and are sat waiting for opportunities to add themselves to your schedule. They can afford to work with you and find joy in buying from you. They are the ones who will take responsibility for their own results whilst valuing the environment and support you have provided. They know you have delivered excellence and the environment from which to strive, and then go and do the rest with real motivation towards their goals. Often, giving you a beaming testimonial afterward.

I have been **so blessed with dreamy clients**. So much so that when 2022 offered up a few non dreamy ones, I was thrown into a state of temporary shock!

You will hear the term, "Ideal client," a lot in our industry, and although it really is an overused phrase, I invite you to listen to it again, focusing mainly on the "Ideal" part.

If you come to me and say, "She's my ideal client but she is too scared to invest right now," that means she is not your ideal client. It means she may be your ideal client one day, but like a juicy avocado she has not yet ripened enough to fulfil this particular of her destiny.

The problem with being visible is we often go into major audience build mode just before a launch. We will try our best, 6 weeks, sometimes 12 weeks ahead of time, to meet new people, because we *need* people then. We think it is okay to neglect them the rest of the time, but the truth is, you should be focusing your attention on audience building every single day.

I'm talking about the important stuff, like actually having conversations and making connections. Always working in the background of your business, bringing new people in all the time and not just so you can sell to them. So that the relationships can be enriching both ways, and for many more valuable purposes than just the sell, sell, sell.

Some online gurus will tell you to: ALWAYS BE SELLING .... A, B, C
I am going to suggest instead, that you ALWAYS BE CONNECTING... A, B, C

We want to be able to nurture that process, so that we can grow our audience base in a non-icky fashion, and it's extremely important that we can first recognise and know who those dreamy clients are for us.

Now, if you have ever done ideal client work, you will probably be sick to the back teeth of this same conversation. The same advice and the focus on this same area. I get it. But know there is not one multi-millionaire I have worked with, who does not regularly review and update their ideal client, dreamy client, marketing demographic, consumer data - literally whatever you want to call them, regularly.

Now, I like to call my audience Pretties. You don't have to have purchased from me to be a Prettie, but most have in some way or form. You may have given me money for my support, you may have given me stars on a video. You may have given me your time in a comment, Often there is an exchange.

The reason why this is important, and why we're lovingly guiding ourselves back to ideal client again, is because you really need to know who they are, and more importantly, what they are feeling.

If you're not sure who it is that you want to work with, or you're not sure who it is that you want to attract, it's

THE AUDIENCE ATTRACTION METHOD

very, very difficult to build an audience. *If you speak to everyone, you speak to no one*, and the only business that should be going after "general public" audiences are pubs and supermarkets really. *(potentially cheese brands - .... everyone loves a bit of cheese).*

Let's say you have an ideal client and you know them well. You know that they are the type of person that is spending up to eight hours a week on LinkedIn. Fabulous bit of data that's going to illuminate which social platform to prioritise based on their active behaviours online.

A key decision in your marketing plan may be that you want to be going to LinkedIn rather than Instagram or Twitter or Facebook.

What other behaviours can you be sure of? Are they the type of person who reads lots of articles? If yes, you want to be making sure that you're actively going into the comment section of those articles on LinkedIn, you automatically have a map and a pathway from you to your ideal client.

If you don't know that they like articles, you don't know that they're on LinkedIn. You don't know what kinds of things they like reading, you don't know what behaviours they have online, you are totally blind to finding your ideal client. This is where so many businesses luck out. Because before they even start, they have no idea who they are trying to speak to.

Remember when I said I am not keen on general advice. Well, every social guru with a Tiktok account will put out content that will seem "helpful," and some really are. But as true slaves to the industry we are in, we also understand what people think they want, and how to abuse the system to grow our own following. That's right, those of us with the know-how, find it very easy to manipulate, and it is an ethical choice whether we do or not. You can probably tell I chose the good side!

For instance, I could create a Tiktok or Reel, "Do this in 5 days to gain 6000 new followers". It would be a hit. It would be an out and out manipulation of the truth, and very close to a lie.

"Get more leads on Instagram" is more my style, which is why you can never call what I give you "General advice." To tell the total truth I must debunk some of the tosh that's floating about between crowd shared opinion and optimistic rumour.

This is the same with ideal client, what is public? And what is a qualified lead?
You are looking at the Rule and trying to find the exception to it.

If you have 20k audience members (followers) on public, a small percentage may (out of sheer luck) be ideal clients. Say 2000 of them. Out of those 2000, you may have 200 that engage. That leaves 20 of them in the potential buying sphere (only 3% of our audiences are ready to buy at any given time) which may give you a sale of 0.6 of a person.

If you have 20k audience members and they are all on your ideal client spectrum, then it is literally a completely different game. 3% of that audience is 600 people and if you convert at 10% then that's 60 people. If you sell something that is £1000 per person that is £60k in your bank.

This is why this book may be one of the best things you ever bought for your business. Don't chase the numbers of public, cultivate actual connections with people on your ideal client spectrum.

Not all will be bullseye perfect matches, but even if they are, on the outer levels, there is an opportunity to nurture and be able to convert them when they are ready, and in that 3%.

Marketing used to be done in a way that was, as many eyes as possible, focus on the number, and don't get me wrong, there's some truth to it. We want many eyes on us, but we want a high number of the right eyes!

If you were to stick one of my courses in a group of female entrepreneurs for £50 there would be a frenzy. Which we sometimes do and I love it.

Stick one of my courses in a group of dudes who work construction and they would laugh me out of the room. They aren't my demographic and I am not theirs either.

There is a match to be made here, like business matching and dating.

When you get to the point that you know your people and

you're already building a fantastic client base, it gets easy. Anything you do once, you can do a thousand times. Once you have met one ideal client, it's just about expanding on that.

So before we go chasing audiences of 20,000 plus, let's scale back. Right now, what you're looking for, is one or two really fantastic, amazing, niched clients that can be brought into your world so that you can learn key things.

Important to note:

*Where you found them
*How they reacted to your connection
*How easy it was to work with them
*What about them makes you sure they meet your ideal client criteria.

Six Figure businesses can be made on as little as 20 clients. So audience attraction might be a situation for you, where you don't need that many people to get it off the ground.

We don't want big numbers if it is general public. First and foremost, you want quality. And then once you know what you need, you can expand on those big numbers and duplicate and duplicate and repeat and repeat. That's where businesses go from naught to 60.

Without that vital information, we can't possibly know what we're looking for, you'll easily find a lot of wolves in sheep's clothing. People who look like ideal clients, speak like ideal clients, and make you believe that perhaps they'll be an ideal client.

You need to be able to review and identify these people

before you get too deeply into a business relationship with them. There is an air of experience that is required here, so first and foremost know that there is some beauty in the benefit of the doubt. However, the more you're interacting with your actual dreamy clients, the more you will be able to tell when somebody is a dreamy client, or when somebody is just masquerading as one.

If you have Facebook or LinkedIn groups that you allow people in as part of a nurture funnel, you're going to notice that there are some people in your group that look like ideal clients. They're qualified to a certain degree, you let them in and there is optimism, but they're only ever there for the free hors d'oeuvres, right?!

They're the ones that never buy anything from you, will take up discovery call after discovery call with no intention of putting their money where their mouth is. Just getting some more free resources. It is important to note that they look like, one day, if you nurture them just right, they might buy something from you. And yet they still never have, and I am sorry to say, often they never will.

This is the kind of thing that you need to keep an eye on in terms of your focus, your energy, and how much time you are spending with these people.

Now remember, we were talking about the messaging, the approach, and the lead. And when you are considering how to build this attraction with your audience, you're going to be doing that because you need the valuable data. The valuable data that will help you to build a picture of who it is that you want to be working with, where you can find them and how you can nurture them in an efficient way, to be able to get through that sales process.

I should also warn you that once you get an idea of who your dream clients are, and almost all of you will have an interpersonal emotional connection with them, you will find that these people are REALLY your people. I can tell you there is no one better in the universe than my pretties. You could include them in any family dinner and they fit right in like family, because they are cultivated on shared values and ethics. As audiences go, you may fall in love with yours and that is okay!

The way I feel about my pretties has allowed me to centre their needs at the right priority for my business. When you have a true connection it's very difficult for you to not have fruitful land joyful relationships that are stemmed in purpose and your core beliefs. It is an addition to your personal life in such a beautiful way and it doesn't replace it. It enhances it because every facet of your life now has positive relationships in it.

To achieve all this however, you need valuable data, because you are essentially looking for your..., for your people, your audience, your soul clients. It becomes a really, significant event, not just for your business, but often for you, personally.

Base points for all, on an ideal client journey, are looking at demographics. You need to paint a picture of who somebody might be, and what stage of their life they may be at.

It may seem boring and simple, but we are absolutely building an imaginary client from the ground up. To do that, we're looking at their age, we're looking at their lifestyle. Their life choices, their hobbies, their gender, their postcode if it is relevant.

For instance, with lifestyle, if you were a health coach, you're not going to be looking for somebody who isn't in the health space yet and needs your advice to get healthy. One of the most horrendous marketing trends of the 2000's has been fitness coaches slipping into the DMs of people who look overweight or unfit in their profiles; to suggest they can help them. This is the opposite of good marketing and shows a super high lack of ideal client work.

In that space, you're looking at people who are newly into health or really enjoy health, high performance and keeping fit. Perhaps they have made a decision themselves and have joined groups for support or they have consumed some great tips. The people who are "IDEAL" will not have to be convinced. They're already on the path to someone like you. You are just participating in the end point of their already established decision.

"I am going to get fit," is totally different to, "That lady said I need to get fit."

Ideal clients are motivated to move in the direction of what you are offering.
They are already hungry and looking for a restaurant. You are not kidnapping them in the street and running away with them. You are merely offering an open door and a menu, perhaps some free bread.

You might be surprised by what you believe a demographic will tell you. Sometimes one will offer you more. For instance, if you know about a family dynamic, you may assume that a single mother, with five children, perhaps isn't in your affordability range. You might determine that asking her to spend 10,000 pounds with you for a mastermind, wouldn't be ideal for her. You may think that investing the eight hours a day, for five days every week, wouldn't work for her and you might be right.

But does your ideal client already have money? Do they come from generational wealth? Are they an exceptional entrepreneur with a budget for what you are offering? Does that lady have a nanny or are all her 5 kids in school now, leaving her free to invest both time and focus into that mastermind?

Don't do surface level demographic building for your ideal client. Go long, go deep, and think of all the different angles of a person.

If you're a careers coach, and you only work with senior management, then you need to know whether they're senior management or not, seems simple, but just being senior management, doesn't sufficiently cover the motivation to improve oneself.

Maybe you must match that, with someone who likes to invest in themselves, or someone who reads self-development books.

Perhaps you want to connect with people who consider themselves lifetime learners.

Some of us never wanted school to end, we just wanted the autonomy to learn about the things that truly interest us.

Maybe that person needs a certain level of intrinsic motivation, like the type that being overlooked and undervalued can give you?

There is so much more to a person than the base demographics.

You can look at behaviours, locations, and everything in between, but I urge you not to ignore what I believe to be the most important one.

Emotions.

AND

Emotional intelligence.

I don't want to offend anybody, but there are people out there that need to have both emotional intelligence and potentially a level of actual intelligence, to be able to identify the benefits of working with you.

You need to know where they are on the sliding spectrum of human feels and actual intelligence and this can become a marker for you to understand your market further.

To buy this book you have already revealed a level of intelligence to me. To know you want to learn more in this particular subject tells me volumes about you as a person! It shows me that you are savvy, you are acutely aware of successful business practices. That you are able to evaluate yourself, to the point of what may be lacking in your knowledge. That you hold space for yourself, in pursuit of closing that gap in your intellect and that you are actively making moves to improve yourself, business, and lifestyle.

Or you are my mum, and you just bought the book to support me. Hi mum!

The thing is when you are working with someone in the future, you want to know that they have the ability to comprehend you.

It is communication yes, but it is comprehension also.

I could take 6 "Dave's" off the street and stick them in a room and talk all day about using the digital landscape to build real human to human connection. How many "Dave's" would actually understand it? Probably none of them, knowing what I do about "Dave's."

This is not me suggesting, that somebody might not be clever enough to work with you per-se, more so that not everyone could possibly be in the right conditions to receive what you deliver.

I'm going to suggest that you put your selfish hat on please, just for a moment. I know it feels unnatural. Just pop it on for a moment and think about what's really right for you.

Remember "IDEAL"

These dreamy clients should be the people that do understand, value you, adore you, pay your invoice on time or early. They are the ones who thank you and leave you an amazing testimonial before they leave. And then if we're going to be completely honest, come back next month to work with you again. Think about that type of experience you want, for yourself too.

What area of emotional intelligence do they need to be at, to fully appreciate what you are offering them?

If you look at it from your ideal client spectrum, from your lens, you'll be able to figure out your ideal client and where you need them to be. You can evaluate if the intelligence level is going to make this partnership achievable?

Where are they at in their learning journey? Can they achieve what you want to help them to achieve? Are they going to come in, be nice and easy, breezy, and enjoy it and get it? What sparks joy for them?

It is really good for you to know this about them in terms of building your content. What makes them super happy and what makes them super frustrated. Then how can you speak to both situations leaving them better than you found them?!

This is the area, of that nurture sequence, that you're at in terms of not just speaking to their need but speaking to the actual person.

Profiling

What is a profiling plan? Think of yourself for a moment as a bit of a, I won't say stalker, but an investigator. You're a private investigator and you want to be profiling people who fit your dreamy client list, do you know enough about them to find them online?

Where can you find them? And where / what is your in?

If somebody wanted to find me, they could probably find me in all the social media groups that are on Facebook for instance.

They could find me in the comments section of other entrepreneurial blogs and on other people's entrepreneurial PR, because I do go and support people when they are in PR.

You could find me in some really random places too. I really love playing Tomb Raider.

Now, most people that would have me on their ideal client list, may not ever dig deep enough to know that about me, and may not know that on an evening, me and the kids and my husband will play Mortal Kombat on the PlayStation five. That I love Tomb Raider and may be commenting on any given forum about how to find the additional ammunition in the jungle that I need to fight the illuminati. You could probably find me in those spaces if you profiled me correctly. There are subtle hints to all my little nuances as a human.

When you have profiled somebody, and you know a lot about them, and those little details, they go beyond your references of niche and into the human part of identification.

It doesn't hurt for you to know those little things, and to understand all the different elements of a person, so that you can really use that to your advantage when you're trying to find people online.

I'd love for you to consider some random ideal client facts for yourself. Give yourself a little mental fact about your ideal client that you already fully know is relevant.

All these little random facts build a person in your mind. Some of us call them Avatars and they are super handy in marketing and messaging because they are the tin can you are throwing your weighted bean bag at, when you write your content or build a new service or product.

My avatar when I first started, used to be called Sophie, and Sophie and I, had a great time. At a certain point in my business, I began to outgrow Sophie a little, so now she's called Freya. She's been Freya for a good few years actually. She gets an upgrade when I do.

Freya is the embodiment of probably somewhere in the region of about 10,000 women now. This just gives all of us as a company, as a team, as a brand, somebody to talk about in terms of collectively creating the ideal client and dreamy client experience. Freya is the person that we're helping every day. You may not realise it but by buying this book, you are a Freya.

Freya is the person that I am looking to help every day. It makes it simple and very, very clear for everyone. Even if you just consider that clarity from a mindset perspective, you can see the benefit in this exercise.,

What is it that I need to do to help Freya today? It allows you to get that great kind of strategy and clarity in knowing what to be spending your focus on.

So let me tell you a little bit about Freya. Freya is super, super intelligent. That doesn't mean that she understands; how to code, build a website or rocket science necessarily, but she has smarts. She is emotionally intelligent, and she's intelligent in the ways of life experience. She has some depth to her, often overlooked. She's the person in the room that probably should be given the microphone but is quite often the person who watches as the microphone gets passed to somebody else right in front of her nose.

She's incredibly passionate and she's ready to act. She appreciates learning, she's got a zest for life, and she's no longer waiting her turn.

She doesn't want to wait anymore. She's comfortable financially, but she does have goals and dreams over all sorts of different things in her life. Dreams to do with, obviously earning more and doing more of the things that set her soul on fire. But more importantly, she's interested in creating a level of success for herself, that perhaps affords her some life changes that she doesn't currently have.

She has a realistic view of business. I know that she won't come to me and think that she's going to spend eight hours with me and walk away a millionaire at the end of the session.

My ideal clients know that work needs to be done. They know that they need to invest in themselves. They know that they need to provide themselves with the right resources and environments to grow. They are heart centred, and often, not always, spiritual on some level.

What's fantastic about my dreamy client Freya is that they recognise opportunities and act on them. You can probably see why attracting this type of client has made everything for me so much easier. People don't add these kinds of traits to their avatars very often but there is confidence in knowing that if you are a Freya, you wouldn't turn down the opportunity to work with me. That is a very simple but powerful qualifying factor.

I invite you to add this to your ideal client avatar. Always look for the people who recognise opportunities. Consider somebody who's going to be willing to listen to you and take what you're going to say with the respect that it deserves. Perhaps your new product is perfect for them. Do they trust you when you tell them about it? Or do they think you are just trying to sell, sell, sell. Freya, for instance, knows that I wouldn't just offer it and is excited to learn more.

What I love about her, is she can see through fakers. I think every single person in the online space will have looked at somebody online and not been sure if the truth is there or if you are buying into "A veil." Because Freya is smart, it is even better for me when she endorses me. People trust her because she has the fakers pegged. When she recommends me, it holds clout. That's something that you cannot buy!

Now, these things allow me not only to go and find people that are my ideal client, but they also allow me, when generally meeting people, to identify my ideal client quickly and efficiently. And with some joy, I can spot a Freya a mile off. Because all my messaging, all my content, all of the things that I talk about in my outward visibility is for her, she can spot me easily too.

That's why this is so important. So when you look at the spectrum of dreamy client, you're going to have that bull's eye area which is your perfect fit. Your Freya, this person is your person, you and they are aligned in values, work ethic and results.

Not everybody that fits, is a perfect fit, hitting bullseye, but you will find those that are a good fit. where there is a relationship to build on. They're still **an** ideal client, they're just not a **perfect fit.**

Then on the outskirts of that, you get your next outer band, which are people who may fit many of your criteria but are not ready yet.

These people are not in the 3% of your audience, ready to buy, but they are absolutely worth nurturing. Don't let them pass you by.

People who are your ideal client, are the people of course that spend money with you. Absolutely. But you're going to get people who fit your ideal client band, and they sit in the outer band for some time, or they might never spend a penny with you. When it comes to business strategic focus, you are not going to spend too much time on the outer band, beyond your normal free resource and funnel strategies.

These people are lovely and valued but cannot monopolise your time when compared to paying clients. When it comes to interpersonal relationships and connecting with other human beings, do not discount them as no value. They are still very valuable and if you can, help them, as often as you can for free, without an agenda, so long as it is not to the detriment of your business. They're still your people and may become your biggest cheerleaders.

Not everyone will buy from you, but you can still make an impact.

When it comes to your audience, if you notice you have somebody new, who's just arrived at your network, don't try selling to them. It doesn't work. On a niche scale where you're looking for ideal client, you're looking for a good experience, and you want to make sure that's what they have. A good experience. Cold, pushy, and desperate never works and can damage your relationships with your other dreamy clients too.

People are watching, even if you have no evidence they are.

Remember you can't measure every single thing, metrics are great, but you can't measure the lurker that doesn't give the technology anything to work with, in terms of collection.

At the middle of all these demographics, one of the most important things that I want you to consider is core values. If you have a strong belief system, that might be a core value to you. If you're a raging feminist, that might be a core value for you.

How does that person feel about the important aspects of life? And what are the things that create that bond between you and your ideal client?

Go and find them, and then chat to them. Go and make a business friend. You just have to talk to them. It is human behaviour; we want to connect with each other. So try not to worry too much about the marketing spiel that tells you that you have to give an elevator pitch in every comment section, just go and find them and answer some questions.

Elevator pitches and long introductions do have a time and place. But first and foremost, just go and find that human, that you're going to connect to, and say "hey."

Remember to think about the groups that they would join, those hobbies, the locational areas that you can go to, the membership groups that they may be in. And those shared interest groups, as well as the business-to-business groups, you know, the ones that are like UK, female entrepreneurs, and all those types of things, and ask engaging questions.

CHAPTER SIX
– LISTEN

In order for you to understand your audience in a way that allows you to serve them you must Listen really effectively.

To the things they say and that which they do not.

Go to your audience and give them PLENTY of opportunities to talk about themselves.

Then shhhhhhhhhhhhhhhhh

DAWN BETH BAXTER

CHAPTER SEVEN - CONTENT IN THEORY

Before we get too deep into it lets bust a little Jargon, shall we?

Copy

Let's have a bit of a natter about what we mean by "copy" in marketing. First of all, we are talking about words or text as you may prefer to call it. But copy isn't JUST words. Picture this: you're at a market, and a friendly vendor is trying to sell you a bag of juicy, delicious apples. He tells you all about the care that goes into growing them, how they're the perfect balance of sweet and tart, and maybe even shares a personal story about his grandmother's apple pie. Essentially, he's painting a picture with words to entice you to buy those apples.

That's essentially what copy is in the world of marketing. It's the words that marketers use to communicate a message about a product or service, whether it's on a website, in a brochure, on a billboard, in an email or even a social media post.

Good copy is like a friendly chat that grabs your attention, stirs your emotions, and convinces you to take some action – like buying those juicy apples. It's more than just explaining what a product is or what it does. It's about creating a story, connecting with the reader's needs or desires, and convincing them why this product or service is just the thing they've been looking for.

To put it simply, copy is the voice of a brand in written form. It's how a business communicates with the world, delivers its message, and engages with customers. So the next time you see some text on a website or an advertisement, remember, that's not just writing - it's copy, doing its job to draw you in and make you feel something.

Caption

Now, let's dive into the world of "captions" in marketing. Picture yourself in a gallery, looking at a beautiful painting. It's lovely, isn't it? But there's a little plaque next to the painting that gives you more insight into the artist's thoughts, or the painting's history, making the painting even more special and meaningful.

In the context of marketing, a caption serves a similar purpose. When we talk about captions, we usually refer to the written text that accompanies an image or video on social media platforms like Instagram, Facebook, or

LinkedIn. It's a bit like that informative plaque in the gallery - it gives the image or video a bit of context, and helps the audience understand the message the brand is trying to convey.

Think of captions as the opportunity to tell a story, explain the context of a post, or ask your audience a question. A good caption can make your audience laugh, think, or feel some kind of emotion that leads them to engage with your post – by liking, commenting, sharing, or even clicking through to your website.

So, in essence, a caption is the marketer's chance to add their voice to the visuals. It can transform an interesting picture into a memorable post that leaves an impact on the audience. It's the cherry on top that gives your visual content a little extra oomph!

So the next time you're scrolling through your social media feeds and stop to read a caption, remember, it's not just there for decoration - it's a critical part of the storytelling!

Touchpoints

In marketing, a touchpoint refers to any interaction a customer or potential customer has with a brand, product, or service. These can happen before, during, or after they purchase something. For instance, a touchpoint could be seeing an advert on TV, chatting with customer service, receiving an email newsletter, browsing a website, or using the product itself.

Why are touchpoints important, you ask? Well, every touchpoint is an opportunity for a brand to make an impression - to show what they stand for, how they're different, and why you should choose them over others.

They help shape the customer's overall experience and perception of a brand.

So the next time you interact with a brand, whether it's clicking on their website, opening an email from them, or walking into their store, just remember - these are all touchpoints, and they're all part of your journey as a customer.

The touchpoints we are able to measure gives us the data we need to calculate our audiences sale potency. They allow us to figure out our conversion rates, our increases or decreases in traffic, interest, engagement and much more.

Social Proof

Imagine you're in a new town looking for a good place to have lunch. You see one restaurant with a queue out the door, while another one is completely empty. Even without knowing anything else, you'd probably think the busy restaurant serves better food. That's because we humans tend to trust the judgement of others. We assume that if lots of people are doing something, they must have a good reason.

In the marketing world, that's what we call "social proof". It's a way of convincing potential customers that your product or service is worth their time and money because other people are happily using it. You might have seen websites showcasing testimonials from happy customers, displaying the number of users or clients, or even featuring endorsements from celebrities or experts. These are all forms of social proof.

In the world of social media, social proof can also be seen

in the number of likes, shares or comments a post has. We are more likely to engage with a post if it already has a lot of interaction.

If you see a business sharing a glowing customer review or stating how many people have bought their product, remember that's not just showing off - that's social proof in action! It's a powerful way businesses build trust and show potential customers that they're in good company.

Content

When we talk about "content" in the world of marketing, think about it like the main course at a dinner party. It's the substantial part that fills you up, gives you something to talk about, and hopefully leaves you feeling satisfied and keen for more.

In marketing, content is essentially all the material that a company creates and shares to engage their audience. This could be anything from blog posts, articles, social media updates, videos, podcasts, infographics, webinars, newsletters, eBooks, and so much more.

But, much like how you wouldn't serve just any dish at your dinner party, good content isn't just about throwing together words or images. It's about providing valuable, relevant information that your audience finds interesting or helpful. You want to engage them, spark their curiosity, solve their problems, or simply make them smile.

Content is one of the ways brands communicate with their customers without directly selling to them. For example, a food company might share delicious recipes, a skincare brand might share tips for a healthy skincare routine, or a travel agency might share beautiful photos and travel guides to different destinations.

All this content serves to create a connection with the audience, builds trust, and nurtures a relationship, much like those memorable dinner party conversations.

Organic/Paid

To help you understand the difference between organic and paid in the context of marketing. Let's think about it in terms of a lovely garden.

In your garden, there are two types of plants: the ones that grow naturally over time, and the ones you plant yourself because you want them to grow quicker, or in a specific spot. Both are valid ways to fill your garden, and both have their pros and cons.

In marketing, the organic approach is akin to the plants that grow naturally. These are activities that don't require a direct payment to be seen or interacted with. For instance, when you create interesting content for your website, or social media, and people find it through a search engine, or their own social feed, that's organic. Like gardening, organic growth takes time, nurturing and patience, but it can result in strong, loyal relationships with your customers.

On the other hand, paid marketing is like planting your own flowers. These are activities where you pay to reach your audience. It can be through search engine advertising, where you pay to appear at the top of search results. Social media advertising, where you pay to reach a larger or more specific audience, or display ads on other websites. The benefits are that you can sometimes get quicker results and can target specific audiences, but it does come with a cost and it isn't an exact science.

Organic marketing is about earning attention naturally, while paid marketing is about buying that attention. Most businesses will use a mix of both in their lifetime, just like a well-rounded garden will have a mix of plants that have grown naturally and ones that have been planted. And remember, whether it's gardening or marketing, the key is to understand what works best for your unique situation and goals.

Click bait

Imagine you're walking down the high street and you see a sign outside a shop that says "Unbelievable deals! You won't believe your eyes!" Naturally, your curiosity is piqued, and you step inside... only to find that the deals are fairly standard, nothing out of the ordinary. You feel a bit miffed, right? You've been drawn in under false pretences.

This is essentially what we mean by clickbait in the digital marketing world. It's a term used to describe sensationalised or misleading headlines, titles, or thumbnails used primarily on the internet. The whole idea is to entice you, the user, to click on a link to read an article, watch a video, or visit a website.

The hook is often an exaggeration, a mystery ("You won't believe what happens next..."), or something that provokes a strong emotion, all designed to pique your curiosity and get you to click. Once you do, you might find that the content doesn't really live up to the hype.

While clickbait can drive traffic to a website or a piece

of content in the short term, it can also disappoint users who feel misled. In the long run, this might damage a brand's reputation and trustworthiness.

Algorithm

I love to demystify the term "algorithm" in the context of marketing. Let's think of an algorithm as a sort of recipe. You know, the kind you'd use to whip up your favourite Victoria sponge cake. It's a set of instructions that tell you what ingredients you need and how to combine them to get your desired outcome.

In the world of visibility, particularly digital marketing, an algorithm is a set of rules that a computer follows to make decisions. For example, when you type a search term into Google, it's an algorithm that decides which websites show up first in the results.

Similarly, social media platforms like Facebook, Instagram, and LinkedIn all use algorithms to decide what content to show in your feed and in what order. It is, in its purest form, Algebra. Algebra that got a bit too big for its boots and let the power go to its head.

These algorithms take into account a huge range of factors. For search engines, they're looking at things like how relevant a webpage is to your search, how many other websites link to it, and the quality of the content on the page. Social media algorithms, on the other hand, consider things like how often you interact with the person or business who posted the content, the type of content being posted, and how recently it was posted.

Understanding these algorithms is crucial for marketers. It helps them figure out how to make their content more likely to be seen and engaged with, whether it's tweaking a website to make it more attractive to Google, or posting content at certain times to get more visibility on Instagram. However, one of the best things you can do to ensure you have a better than average success rate, is not allow yourself to become a slave to the algorithm by ignoring your audiences wants and needs.

When you're taking a stroll through social media land, remember there's an algorithm a little like a maps path finder, working behind the scenes, sorting through heaps of digital 'ingredients,' or laying down bricks to form a path beneath your feet to serve you a personalised 'cake' or "destination" of content.

Engagement

It's a bit like a friendly conversation you have with someone you've just met at a party. You're trying to build a connection, get them interested in what you're saying and make them want to continue the conversation, right?

Similarly, in marketing, "engagement" is a term all about sparking that connection between a business and its customers or potential customers.

It's about creating interactions that are meaningful. This could be anything from encouraging a customer to like or share a social media post, respond to an email, leave a product review, or participate in a survey. The ultimate goal is to create a strong relationship where audience members and potential and actual customers feel valued and want to stick around, much like nurturing a good friendship.

In the age of digital marketing, measuring this

engagement is more detailed than ever. We can look at things like how long someone spends on a website, how many pages they visit, whether they leave comments on blog posts, how often they share content, and so much more. All of this gives us valuable insight into how well we're connecting with our audience and what impact we are leaving behind in every interaction.

It's not about shouting the loudest about your product or service. It's about starting a genuine conversation and keeping that dialogue going in an interesting and beneficial way between both parties. That's the essence and magic of engagement.

When we build content, we tend to do it through a lens of "how will this please people." We do it looking for likes. Looking for approval and hoping often praying that something we share will be taken in by someone who is on our ideal client spectrum.

You may think that giving tips and hints and statistics is a good idea. It might be!

You may think quotes are fun, they are!

But what actually changes your content from "This is nice" to "OMG Yes"?

The idea that we can share national awareness days and box off a full years' worth of "content" makes me want to throw myself out of a window. Although I don't want to continually go back to General advice vs Expert advice, I fear I must.

General advice will tell you to have.

- National awareness days

- Recurring regular themes
- A post per day
- A set certain number of hashtags or to post at 3pm on a Wednesday.
- Content themes and Pillars that don't change.

A general social media strategy may look like this.

1. Motivational Monday
2. Top Tips Tuesday
3. Wins Wednesday
4. Thriving Thursdays
5. Funny Friday
6. Social Saturday
7. Self-care Sunday

Now if you are looking at this with this face...

please don't despair!

Everyone starts somewhere, and I actually love a funny Friday personally, & if you have one of these you probably have a legitimate reason for keeping this in your strategy. That being said the above is not a content strategy, its alliteration.

If you are an absolute beginner, you will do whatever you need to get going and get comfortable and that is okay. What almost always will inevitably happen however, is you will get months or even years in, wondering why your audience growth is slow and your leads are not turning into paid clients.

When you are sitting down to make a plan on how to show up on social media, the best thing you can do to start, is to STOP. That means before you begin, have a think about what expectations and pressures you have already mentally piled on to yourself.

Let me be really honest. Ready.... It comes from a place of love I promise. Okay here you go.

> *It is unlikely that your posts are going to bowl people over straight away. - That's okay*

> *Sometimes no one will show up for your posts, videos, lives, or reels. - That's okay.*

> *You will sit in front of your computer without a word to type or utter because the paralysis of it being perfect will freeze your brain in time - That's not fun, but it will be okay.*

Your content needs to reflect you. You need to be able to find the cross section between where your ideal client starts and you end. Consider emotions once more and instead of set days of the week, think about your audience's life journey and experiences.

For instance, I can post today about how difficult it can be to connect with your ideal client, and that the solution to that would be X,Y,Z. That's because I know how to build audiences and my ideal client needs an audience, but hasn't cracked their own personal brand of audience genius yet.

Each one of you has that, whether you realise it or not. No one is more qualified than you to talk to your audience!

If you think of emotions, you can still build Pillars/ themes but they become much more than just poetic words.

Maybe you will give a mix of

- Common feelings we share.
- Topics that will make their life easier today.
- Emotional support (both positive and negative experiences discussed)
- Polarising content (yes that means not being scared to share how you feel, respectfully mind!)
- Storytelling with a purpose (don't forget the reason it is relevant to your people)
- Inspiration to move action (perhaps also including do now steps)

Consider subjects that build rapport, those that align with your ideal client markers and those that allow people to feel closer in understanding you.

Never forget the power of sharing:

YOUR OPINIONS - YOUR CORE VALUES - YOUR ETHICAL CODE - YOUR BELIEFS.

These are the most powerful connectors and they allow for some incredibly powerful bonds to form.

When you consider building the content, you can use a very simple formula.

Messaging + Media + Platform.

You may want to share emotional support and know that video is the only way to go. Perhaps you have considered that being able to see your facial expressions, tone and body language will allow your audience to connect in a more impactful way. Perhaps your biggest and most engaged audience is on Facebook so you choose to post your video there.

That is the trifecta of content choice based on solid content strategy. With a bit of luck and hard work, that one piece should also fit into a wider strategy for your overall marketing and then again for your overall business goals.

This is a Russian doll situation. Strategy inside strategy inside strategy.

It has been said, that in order for someone to be ready to buy from you, and move into the emotionally open and trusting centre of your audience's brain, you may have to have been seen in an impactful way 50 times or more.

That is why the online space is noisy for entrepreneurs, because no matter how often you think you are showing up, you are probably still being missed by an ideal client somewhere.

The common theme for me to educate you with, is that once again, it's not actually about you. I wonder if you realised when you bought this book, I would so often attempt to take your limelight away? - forgive me, it is for the greater good.

Of course, we are human and sometimes we just want to express ourselves and that's okay!

What I would lovingly suggest is that you have a solid strategy, that gives your audience the main floor space, and then you add your self-expression on. As well as, not instead of, and only after you have your business bases covered.

You want your audience member to see your socials and go, "who me?" because they identify with what you have shared. The more you make it about them, the better.

Remember:

- Relate to where they are in their journey!
- Don't neglect Social Proof, Belief, and Knowledge.
- Clarity on what they get by following you and engaging with you.
- Give them reasons to love you or hate you but never stick in the middle ground.
- Encourage a feeling within them.
- Main character energy time!

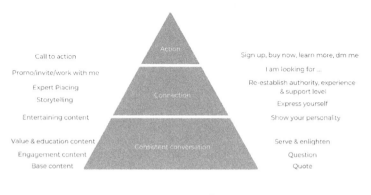

Also consider what messages allow for:

- Brand Awareness
- Building Authority
- Emotional triggers (with a closed ending - we leave people better than we found them rather than poke bruises)
- Consumer safety/trust
- User generated content

When you make a plan to create for your people, remember you are only speaking to your dreamy client. You are giving yourself the opportunity to show all the ways you are a perfect fit for your people and why you should be at the top of their minds when they are in a position to buy.

CHAPTER EIGHT - CONTENT IN MOTION

A universal mistake I see when people come to me for support in the way they are showing up online, is that it is easy to disrespect the amount of time, energy and thought that is required to create a well-rounded messaging strategy.

The content you put out in the world can be "on the fly" or "in the moment as you feel it" sure, but it should never be rushed, fumbled, or lacking a direction that fits into your wider plan.

Yes, inspiring, uplifting or simply being a safe energy for your people today, still counts as part of your wider nurture and probably purpose in terms of your bigger picture plan.

The "Oh gosh I haven't posted in 2 weeks so I will share this picture of my sandwich" is the worst way to go about this as a practise for your business.

I personally have worked with many successful and wealthy people and giants of the luxury brand market, who have globally impactful messages or massive global followings and perception sway. So much so, that it can make your hair stand on end and have you reconsider the meaning of life.

They have ways of altering people's reality.

Please know, that they too have done this same thing at some point, and you are not alone! So when you think you are failing, know you are not. You just haven't nailed your full direction yet and that does take time or a deeper understanding such as you have found in this book.

That being said, now we will know better - we can do better, right?

Here are some things your content should never be:

Rushed

All about you

Including any Bad techniques or too much promo

Shame language

Negative mental health prompts

Boring

Here are some things your content should be:

Thought out

All about your person (audience/clients/ IC avatar)

Warm, open & inviting

Encouraging

Left on a positive note, or offering options for people to seek support or help if that's not possible

Enjoyable, engaging and interesting

The old adage of "If you fail to plan then plan to fail" is fairly accurate in terms of content being built.

It is a creative task, it is a writing task, it's a marketing task and it's an admin task.

Actually, it's a sales task and branding task. So why is it not on your calendar?

Maybe, add that as a task?

If you take one thing from this book, of course I hope there will be many more than one, but even if just one, please let it be this. **You need to plan in planning it in. Then you need to plan creating it, building it and scheduling it.** They are not all the same job or task and they don't rely on just one skill. Which is why we procrastinate over it.

There are tools to help you - of course, and we will address them later but for now the biggest tool you should be learning to use is, **giving yourself enough time to perform this action** in your business well. Or finding the budget so you can outsource to someone who can.

First - find 10 mins in your diary. Got ten minutes now? Excellent! Go to your schedule/ calendar and plan for the next 12 months:

*When you will create your content

*How often

*In what conditions

It may look like:

The first of every month, once every month and in my favourite coffee shop.

It may look like:

Once every two weeks, rolling biweekly until September, in bed with the cat.

Commit to the time. Plan to reoccur. Cultivate your space for optimum productivity.

For me, building content needs to happen in quiet. I am an internal reflector, even as I type this, I have my own voice (or a strange version thereof) reading out each word that graces this chapter. I love music. The part of my brain that creatively writes and emotively connects really likes music too. Feed her music and she is too busy to build a graphic, edit a video or write a caption. I must starve her of outward funky distraction and force her inward to get the results I want.

If white noise helps great, add it in. If doing it on a Sunday is your jam then fab.u.lous. But what you must be wary of is attempting it under the wrong conditions.

There is no room for stress, overwhelm, rushing, waves of mass distraction or anything that may stop you from being able to submerge yourself into the messaging you are going to portray.

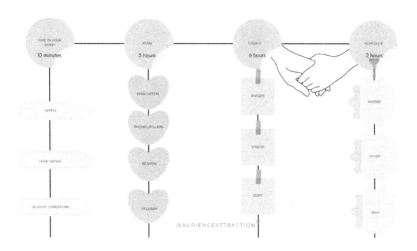

Once you have set the time in your diary and you're ready to actually plan, rather than plan to plan, you will create a structure. Give yourself at least three hours for this. Longer if you are a deep thinking, consider every aspect type.

Even if you are impulsive and a "get it done and out" already like me, give yourself those three solid hours. Then if you complete it sooner reward yourself with a cookie or a nap or something wonderful like that!

During that time, you are going to nail down:

- *How often you want to show up online*
- *Which themes/pillars/messages will feature*
- *The reason you are tying things back to*
- *The delivery method you're choosing for those pieces of content*

For instance, this could look like:

- *3 times a week on Facebook, 2 on Instagram and 1*

on linked in.
- *Storytelling about how long it has taken me to be able to share my work in new ways, inspiration to help my audience know they can do it too, emotions around being confident in vulnerability.*
- *Leading into launching my book on visibility and showing up for your audience authentically*
- *2 graphics, 2 photos, a carousel post and a video (reel)*

Once you have got that in your back pocket you then need to actually make the content, which I would always suggest setting 6 hours or a working day aside for (especially if you are building a month in one go).

This is the time where you set up the camera and record yourself, or head over to your brand shoot file and choose the pictures you want to share. You might log into Photoshop, Illustrator or Canva and make yourself a graphic. You then write your captions, research, and choose your hashtags and get everything ready, preferably in a content "bank".

Once this is complete, you give yourself 2 hours to schedule it all in using whichever scheduler you like the best.

The nature of this allows you to automate posts going out, so that you don't have to be on the hook to show up for your audience!

I skipped over the term "Content Bank" and I really shouldn't because having one of these is a genius move. Please don't trust your content safety to a scheduler or a social media platform only. Give yourself the safety of holding all of your business assets somewhere where you can always lay your hand on them as you need to!

We just worked out that a months' worth of content may cost you a minimum of 11 hours and 10 minutes. Don't waste that time invested in your creations as they become assets to repurpose and use again!

When you create, don't worry that every post won't be a showstopper. Your audience needs time to calmly consume also. A way of doing this is what we lovingly call "Base content".

Base content is your messaging that is true for any season of your business. It is the type of messaging that would fit in to your strategy no matter what you are doing or selling. It allows people to subtly rely on your consistency and for you to seamlessly sink into their subconscious without being detected. If you use your messaging for good and not evil, this is totally acceptable to do.

Base content should always include a healthy dose of audience building in it, (see chapter four) because you want to be inviting new leads into your business all the time. The only time base content is abandoned is during Launch content.

Launch content is more powerful, it requires a strength of direction. It is unapologetic and when done right, it's like the peak of a gentle rollercoaster. A nice steady incline reaching a peak that plateaus and then gently floats back down to the ground.

Launch content however has one goal and all the messages of that content should be rivers that lead back to one main sea. We will call this the sales sea! When we execute Launch content, we have to deactivate our internal ick for selling (if you have that, I don't! I bloody love selling) and allow yourself to be a bit salesy to get those rivers back to the sales sea. You see?

Launch, especially live launch, should disrupt all other forms of content and you should never have more than two main themes running at the same time. Do not give multiple options of interest, filter all the attention towards the area of your business that is getting it's 15 minutes, (two weeks or so) of fame.

Evergreen products can also be added in as launch style strategy or you can pop them into your normal monthly strategy, but be aware - shared too often they may become subliminal content that people consume but do not take action on. You can fade too far toward the back of someone's mind and we want to be at the front of the back really.

Give each post a deeper underlying reason to be consumed. Let me share one of my really old ones that performed well.

You can see this is a storytelling post, there was a very humble and simple visual story told with the image. The overall message was inspirational with a side order of "relatable" and the caption allows for me to show my personality, my honesty, and my gratitude all in one go. It also gives my audience the opportunity to engage and talk about themselves.

When you are building your content, give yourself lots of opportunities to pack it with subliminal value and messaging - you won't regret it.

People want to know you are human. Show them and give them permission to do the same.

Ethical practice

Ethics and Marketing haven't always been friends. In fact, despite the best efforts of agencies like mine, the relationship, to this day is still what you could consider to be "strained" at best.

When you are trying to build a business and an audience it becomes really easy to forget your values and ethics in pursuit of getting there faster. Many of us have thought about the fact that maybe it is okay to cold DM someone to reach out and sell to. We may have joined engagement pods or bought followers.

We don't need to know - but you know.

When it comes to icky sales practices that may seem effective, I can promise you that the quick wins you may (or may not) see today will cost you in the long run.

I say it is better to opt for longevity.

Let's look at each shady practice and promise not to use them, okay?

Okay! I know you wouldn't anyway prettie but let's be aware of them so we can spot them a mile off!

Engagement pods

Engagement pods are not as popular as they used to be, but what used to happen, is that you would be invited into a group who would all have businesses, you would agree to like and comment on a certain amount of people within the group. These seem like a good idea because the socials would pick up on many people liking and commenting on your post and push you out further. In theory it is an algorithm hack and a kindness to fellow small businesses. Often the support of others was the draw to do it.

The problems with this are endless though.

1. You are obliged to use vital engagement time with people who you will not buy from and who will not buy from you.
2. You are training the socials to show your content to the people who aren't interested in you and are only commenting because they are obliged to.

After a while everyone notices their engagement has

dropped despite the same 10 people commenting on their posts each day. They begin to notice sales dropping and get resentful of continuing for others when it isn't working for them.

It seems like a small practice, but depending on how deep you go with this, can determine if your accounts will survive it. We have had to help clients start from absolute scratch before, because they had tanked their possibilities of reaching genuine ideal clients in a permanent way.

Cold prospecting

This one is super easy. Dropping into someone's DMs and pitching to them off the bat, is the online equivalent of the door-to-door salesman, with his foot on your step, stopping you from closing your post-box to his nose. Just because we have the means to access each other in that way, doesn't mean we should abuse that!

It is really important that when you do chat to people, you are not that annoying person who jumped in with both feet.

The other reason is because if you don't know someone, at all, how could you possibly know that what you have to offer is for them? To do this, you have to either offend people or make wild assumptions. It is a throw mud at the wall approach and its tacky.

Client poaching

Client poaching is when someone asks for support in an area where you can help. People flood to the comments to recommend people or pitch themselves. In this situation you want to consider a few things.

Where am I?
If you are a therapist in a group hosted by a therapist, it is totally acceptable to introduce yourself and welcome a chat. However, it doesn't hurt to mention the host politely also.

The host will appreciate you for your professional conduct. The person who needs help will likely be aware of the host and have discounted the possibilities for a variety of reasons (often cost).

The worst thing you could do: would be to be negative about other providers in the room to try and get the business or friend request that person and get in their DMs before anyone else.

Stay calm. Clients meant for you will not pass you by. If you are classy about it, not only will the original person see you, but everyone else will. You will likely incite more inbound DMs by your ability to be professional, helpful, and yet not overly eager.

Negative mindset prompts

If you have ever been through a funnel and seen the prompts to buy the tripwire or the bump in there, you may have seen the popularity of using psychology in sales pages.

This is an area that I am an expert in, but you don't have to be an expert to be able to see what is wrong with negative mindset prompts.

A negative mindset prompt is a sales tactic, using

psychology to coerce you into choosing what the salesperson wants you to choose.

Positive Psychology marketing® May have a statement on a button that says.
"I am ready to change my life". This is positive. Yes, it is a sales button and it says so much more than just "buy me" but it leaves the person feeling empowered, joyful about the purchase and probably pretty chuffed that they have made a key decision to do so.

A negative mindset prompt may have a statement underneath that button that says.

"I am happy to go back to my mediocre existence, rejecting my one true chance to be happy".

Can you see how damaging that could be? Especially to someone who is looking for answers or support. What if that person is already vulnerable?

When hard sales pages are created by sharks, the idea is persuasion but persuasion does not hit you over the head with a bat and throw you in the boot of a car.

James Bond was a master of persuasion and he would command a room with a sparkle in his eye, a well-timed comical pun, and a shaken martini.

Negative prompts show your shade. Your bum's hanging out for all of us to see and it says something not great in terms of integrity and character.

Also, from almost every data report I've seen – it's ineffective in comparison to positive messaging.

Shame language

If you are in beauty, fitness, nutrition, or health, you have a trickier time being able to market to general "pain points" than your standard business.

Sadly, often businesses in these industries (and more) rely on the opposite to push sales.

"Want that bikini bod so you're the one turning your husbands head this summer rather than the barmaid at the all-inclusive" - YAK.

"Sick of looking old and tired"? - YAK

This includes shaming minorities, ethnicities, sexual orientations, and belief systems. If you have to drag someone down to the depths of their self-esteem bucket and make them feel "less than" to sell what you have to offer, then your product or service is lacking.

The amount of people who get DMs with pictures of tummies once flabby and now tight is ridiculous. Its horrendous and again - ineffective.

Blanket friend requesting

Add interesting people, add people to network, add people to continue your chat about how you want to be a fulltime home cat mum - whatever you like. But do not join other people's groups and press "add friend" to everyone in the hope that some of your ideal clients will be in there for you. Be more discerning with your friendship seats.

Friend bait and switch selling

Ever made an online friend and had great conversations with them and then the chat goes off the boil and everyone moves on with their lives, only to have a copy and paste message dropped in your DMs later? That feeling of "oh, so that was why they were friendly". Eeep awkward!

General bait and switch selling

"Join my forever free group for amazing value" - three weeks later, "due to demand I am going to kick out everyone who doesn't pay me £1000 a year to stay in this group."

Keep the free group - start another group for a membership. You can even take away resources or value from the free group if you want, but don't get people in on a promise and then break it. Bad form.

Embellishing, lying or rose tinting to extremes.

This one goes out to all the clients I have fired, because they asked me to make content about multiple 7 figure sales, even after I had seen the back of their Kajabi and they'd barely made multiple 5 figures.

I will never tell, and I am under NDA! but just know that sadly - they are out there. Lying to you (and me)! Not every agency is walking away from 50k+, based on morals and ethics alone.

Rose tinting is something we all do, and it's good to expand the good things in marketing, but let's be aware, that as leaders we have the opportunity to inspire, but also force others to feel less than, if they aren't having experiences like ours.

I love sharing when I travel for instance, but when I am going through some personal stuff that isn't fun, I will also reference it. Don't rose tint everything, show a bit of real so people can see you are a person just like them.

Basic copy and paste DM scripts.

AI before AI - They lack personality and don't perform well. If you are in business-to-business selling, then you have the delight of the person on the other side probably having bought, used or been at the end of the same scripts before.

It sounds like "I don't care, give me all your money" - in fact that may convert better!

They piss off your audience and the platforms. Proper waste of time!

General advice coaches and consultants will tell you they are good. This is off the basis that they work. Which in high volumes for short periods they do. This is why they are used in multi-level marketing and pyramid schemes.

What they cannot do is connect you to your clients in a way that breeds loyalty, repeat custom nor referral.

Launch Content

I know I have spent a decent amount of time now telling you how not to be too salesy with your content. Now I am going to give you the salesy bit.

Your launch content is not audience building content. Your launch content has only one directive but many customer journey steps to sell your thing.

In 2023 the word on the street is that live launching is dead. It isn't and it will never be. Every Black Friday, January sale, July sale and "CLOSING DOWN SALE EXTRAVAGANZA" is a live launch but just named something else.

In the online space, we have curated selling to fit our way, but we haven't really made something new. We have taken a sales psychology as old as your great grandparents (or older) and translated it into a digital age.

Live, or shall we re-identify it as "close" launching, is determined by these key things.

- *Build up*
- *Buzz*
- *Hype*
- *Excitement*
- *Inclusion*
- *Offer open*
- *Sell like your life depends on it*
- *FOMO*
- *Close*

And then the painful part where people ask for the product you just opened because it is perfect for them but they missed the launch.

When Launching there are some rules that are strict and others that are okay to bend.

Most Launches are scrappier than you think and often flexibilities are the difference between thousands in the bank.

I like to consider "If it is right for them, let them in" as my approach.

The barriers are.

- *Can I help them?*
- *Is there a means to make it work?*
- *Risk assessment*
- *Reward assessment.*

The rules I will bend.

- *Bespoke payment plans*
- *Deposit to join with payment plan set out for the following month*
- *Discounts, bundle offers, alumni deals for those who already invested in themselves through me.*
- *Changing payment dates to support needs*
- *Additional throw ins, bonuses, and bespoke bits to support a person joining (each person has a circumstance to be considered)* Be aware with this one, if you do for one, you have to be willing to do for all, for fairness!

The rules I will not bend.

- *Holding spaces without some form of deposit or payment*

- *Lying about the amount of spaces available*
- *Skill swapping places on courses*
- *Reopening after cart close for "an extra day bonus"*
- *Allowing people to join weeks into the course*

Launch content will have a strategy both for outside visibility and inside visibility.

And they will be all about what the reasons are to buy the product. Your organic content should be leaning towards having people in your audience relate to the product needs as often as possible, without leading them to frustration.

It should place you as the authority in being able to solve those problems, and it should support them in finding that you will be offering more and more value for them, before you open up whatever it is your selling!

There are a few things that need to be addressed here.

When you are launching in this way, and it's an annual or biannual event, there should be a MASSIVE buzz in your audience. You should be talking about it months before it happens. You should be sharing your information and content in every possible place repeatedly, without any worries at all. You send multiple emails a week or even a day if needs be, to make sure everyone knows about it.

If you do a challenge launch, you want to entice people in, and offer the breakthroughs and prizes.

If a masterclass, give enough information for someone

really new to your world, to go and action, get some quick wins and then allow the more matured audience member, (someone who's followed you longer - no bearing on actual age) to be enticed to invest in themselves properly.

Even with live podcasts, full day seminars, events, or any other kind of open - close launch, you will do one of two very important things.

- *Activate your audience whilst also raising your profile*
- *Sell your thing.*

Even the audience who join in but don't buy, are closer to working with you. Those that do buy, are in for a treat and it is wonderful!!

When you are only doing this irregularly, you can go all out, full pelt and with no shame. All the audience building content you have added around it, will support it and hold it for you, and when it all closes down, you can go back to it seamlessly restoring equilibrium.

If you have any hang ups about selling, open and close launches will require you to give yourself at least a two weeks "all out" permission pass to really go for it.

If evergreen, and open all the time however, you want to be adding this into your general organic content, casually and regularly, often talking about it to your audience. This is more for awareness than for a push launch – however, you are well within your rights to have a little special offer, or push each quarter, to let people know it is there!

If you are doing a live launch, don't neglect the level of return on investment to get good quality audience nurture and prospecting support, (*ahem, my agency does this as an artform, ahem*), high-quality content such as videos, gifs, graphics, covers, email additions, sales pages - THE WORKS. If you have a budget (sure you do!) then spend some of it on this!

Content will help you sell - but remember it cannot sell for you. It is still on you or your sales team to actually get the clients in the door.

Sales prompts

Sales prompts and calls to action are not the same but they are close. *"DM me"*, works best if you are asking someone to share something that will open a conversation. *"Book in now"*, is brilliant for sales calls or casual chats. *"Buy now"* or *"click here"* are more demanding, and allow you to reach new heights of digital bossy.

So why as humans do we need a prompt? Well, we are easily distracted, we are often prompted in marketing and have become accustomed to it. Sometimes we are not really engaging our brain and we need someone to make it so easy for us to do what is required, that we don't need to think about it.

Sales prompts do need to be direct, clear and offer urgency.

Fear of Missing out (FOMO) and urgency are like conversion automations. They take a person on the fence and highlight the benefits of making a decision. It is fine

THE AUDIENCE ATTRACTION METHOD

during a launch to say things like "Click the link now before we close tomorrow at 10pm" for instance.

You may want to steer away from shame language/ narratives such as "Buy now or watch your competitors take their kids to Disneyland instead of you".

I wish I had made that last one up.

When it comes to sales prompts you must be direct, firm, and clear. Repeat regularly without shame but also be thoughtful about your use of language and what you may be accidentally implying.

Outside of Launch be more casual with sales prompts. This is where "DM me to chat about whether this is right for you", lives and breathes, and often keeps businesses ticking over.

Don't be scared to give your audience a clear understanding of what you would like them to do next. Equally don't tell them what to do all the time. You may be an authority but you don't need to treat them like you are the farm dog and they are sheep - at least not every day!

Audience exhaustion

One of the quickest way for you to tank your content operation is to allow it to be either solely audience build or solely salesy. More people do the latter than the former.

Your strategy IS SO IMPORTANT and your content should always be a driving force in getting that strategy moving, BUT...and this is a JLO, Kardashian sized butt.

Your content should not be a copy and paste of your

158

strategy map. If you are selling to your audience more than one product over and over throughout the year, you will exhaust them.

No matter how many of your products complement each other.

No matter how many of them your ideal clients need.

No matter how much they admire and have connected to you.

Each member of your audience has a sales value, that is true. Some it will be £0.00 ; some it will be £47 and some it could be £80k.

You will get them through whatever their amount is, super quick, if you convert them well.

Others will be stunted because they haven't mentally recovered from their last investment yet.

Some will be confused because they haven't used or been able to identify a return on the last thing they bought.

Regardless of your audience's numerical value to your business, they hold value in deeper ways that shouldn't be exploited through the constant selling. Remember the person behind the paycheck.

Over selling can look desperate and if you are not getting fresh faces in front of your business, you will be selling to the same pool of people over and over and over.

It can make you look like each service or product isn't getting your full attention, and can also confuse your audience as to why there are so many products to choose from.

This is only a problem when it is hammered on your outward visibility.

Inside email lists, groups, and more exclusive spaces allows you to get away with this more than you will in open and public land. If you burn through your audience too quickly and they move on completely, you will have less people who are superfan status to support you in showing your unique selling points, personality, and authority than if you didn't.

Selling all the time works for big companies who are advertising with budgets in the thousands and therefore replenishing numbers easily behind the scenes.

When we teach our Social Media Managers during their certification process, I always reference this, because this will be a defining moment for an *ethical social support*.

Clients who are being disingenuous, requesting for unethical practices to be performed or are exhausting their audience *need to be told*.

They need to know how *harmful for their brand and reputation* it is.

I always suggest having the hard conversation to support them in the way they need it, even if they don't want it.

The question always arises.

"Will we lose clients?"

My response, **"Not good ones."**

CHAPTER NINE - YOUR STRATEGY

Before we get this chapter and party thereof started, I do need to caveat this one thing. If you have the means to outsource the building of your strategy to a social media strategist, multi marketer like myself, please do.

In the formative years of your business your survival past the 3-year mark and the 5-year mark will highly depend on the amount of client conversions you can get and the way your customer journey works.

A good strategist will align your audience building into your overall digital marketing strategy, as well as your potential to maximise client liaison and satisfaction to its fullest.

When you begin, you are without a shadow of a doubt, making moves that will support your growth quickly or making moves that will delay a process that doesn't need to be delayed. There are many entrepreneurs that struggle to start the building blocks of their own pathway because they have not yet understood the lay of the land.

Your roadmap can be created yourself, but if you have the opportunity to have insider help at the very beginning, you will find it a lot easier and likely cheaper in the long run.

After years of following a strategy, you will learn enough and know what is best for your audience. You may need support in other areas such as tapping into new audiences, re-engaging ones that have gone quiet etc, but by then the income will already be flowing.

Don't buy cheap and buy twice. Either test a lot out for free (i.e., not really free because it will be you that does it) or get a strategist in to help you get off the ground in a more profound way.

Building your strategy must not be just about all the things you want to sell and when you want to be on holiday. It needs to be a committed relationship with your Brand identity also.

Before you start building anything, think about how you want to be seen and understood. I always suggest starting with slogans, phrases or things that identify you as a fully established brand.

For us, it is in the small things we repeat. For instance, you, aka my audience and clients are called "Pretties". My first business that started the whole business journey for me was called "pretty home prints". Which is where Pretties came from. I intentionally spell it my way to further identify it as part of my brand awareness.

There are personality traits that hold weight also, such as my eyelashes! You will even see them featured in this book. Pretties know that if there are no lashes on, something is very very wrong and help needs to be alerted.

It has become as well-known as our shades of pink and our comical reels!

We also have slogans I say regularly. They are all natural, but they are used and therefore have been attributed.

> *"It's a marathon, not a race".*
> *"Fur coat and no knickers".*
> *"Forget ABC - Always Be Celling..... ABC = Always be CONNECTING."*
> *"It's about them, not you".*

What would your slogans be? What are things you love that will help your audience identify you?

How do you bring your people in on the action? One of the simplest things I have ever done is to create a Pretties vision board. On this board is a lot of great life experiences. Things that would spark joy, and what I want for myself and for my clients. I would pop a pretties name on a pink, love heart post it, and add her to the vision board.

This way when I share that board on social or in the background of my videos, that prettie, is there with me. She knows she is valued, that she is thought of and now part of the Beyond the Dawn legacy forever. This has been such a joy to portray and it solidifies a genuine gratitude and feeling towards my audience.

Once a prettie, always a prettie!

Building a Strategy for yourself? Okay! Well let's talk about ways you can do that!

One of the places I would suggest starting would be by using a messaging map.

This map allows you to add your key themes and pillars on the top level and then filter them down into more specific pieces of content. The messaging map exercise can help you to make sense of your content thoughts and categorise what is truly going to work for your directive.

It can look like this.

· My audience needs to know how to build and attract a client.

- Video tips on how to find, convert and onboard first 5k client.

- Tips A, B, C - Use of keywords — personal story (storytelling)

Here is an empty one for you:

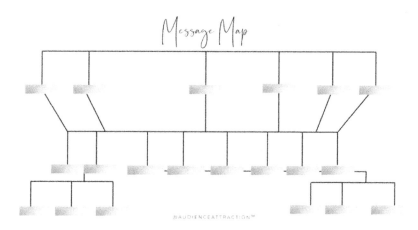

& one that is filled in to make it easier to make your own!

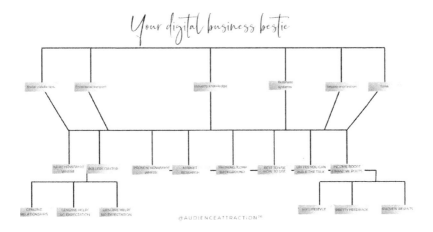

@AUDIENCEATTRACTION™

When you have this part, you can refer back to it regularly for your own source of inspiration. It is really handy!

It takes away so much struggle from trying to be all the things at once and ending up with content paralysis.

Your strategy should be about reaching new people but also about connecting.

A good way to help you with this is thinking about Method acting.

Method acting.

Method acting is an intricate approach to performance that places a high value on realism and emotional honesty. Pioneered by great acting teachers like Lee Strasberg and Konstantin Stanislavski, method acting calls for actors to not just portray, but to live and breathe their characters, often drawing on personal experiences to find parallels and better understand the character's emotional journey.

This is so transformative.

When an actor engages in method acting, they cultivate a profound level of compassion for their character, opening up to feelings and experiences they might not otherwise encounter. This practice can also generate deep, relatable performances because it allows the actor to immerse themselves completely in the character's mindset and circumstances.

It's a beautiful process of empathy, self-discovery, and connection - the heart and soul of acting.

When you build your content strategy you need to be stood in your dreamy clients boots. You need to feel how they feel in that moment.

Like Mary Poppins stepping into the map, you need to be able to embody the moment they are currently in, in their journey.

Think yourself a method actor and start to build what you believe they will be thinking, feeling, and dealing with in their lives.

I also suggest flipping this on its side a little and adding a little extra to this exercise.
Think about how you want them to feel consuming your content.

Maybe they are stressed and now they have read your post and they feel seen, less alone and are giving themselves some self-compassion based on your words, thoughts, and shared feelings.

When I say that connection is the least valued and most precious commodity on the internet, you best believe, you can change the world merely from the other side of your social accounts. You can change how someone feels about themselves, their business, their strengths, their weaknesses - anything.

Yield the power for good and remember there is a real soul on the end of your messaging, not just financial gain.

Psychology in marketing.

I pride myself on putting quality graphic design, the theory of aesthetics, sales psychology, and a knowledge of social media together to build multiple containers, programmes, and courses. The psychology isn't new, it just hasn't been so beautifully accompanied before by methodologies that directly support audience building!

The Audience Attraction Method® embraces the very important part of what we are all looking for, when we are connecting with people online and showing ourselves online too.

We are looking to explore, understand and share our own identity. So much of what we do online now taps into self-expression.

How we share and express ourselves to others forms the basis of our personality

Identity formation involves three key tasks: Discovering and developing one's potential, choosing one's purpose in life, and finding opportunities to exercise that potential and purpose.

A hunger for authenticity guides us in every age and aspect of life. It drives our explorations of work, relationships, play, and prayer. Authenticity is also a cornerstone of mental health. It's correlated with many aspects of psychological well-being, including vitality, self-esteem, and coping skills.

Acting in accordance with one's core self—a trait called self-determination—is ranked by some experts as one of three basic psychological needs, along with competence and a sense of relatedness.

Social psychologist Henri Tajfel conducted pioneering research on prejudice, revealing that people favour those in their own groups, even when those groups are designated randomly, such as by people's preferences for artwork. This research was the basis for Social Identity Theory—that self-esteem is in part derived from group membership, which provides pride and social identity.

This may seem a little baffling but it is really a window into a key area of connection and strategy building for your content.

You want to consider your audiences "**Relatable Objection**s" and then speak to them.

> *Are they scared to invest because they have been burned before?* Speak about it.
> *Do they struggle with mindset?* Talk about it.
> *Will they tell you they are too busy and use that as an excuse to hide from their own potential?* Call them out on it.

In our office we call it the "Relate Weight" and we try to address hard subjects or conversations other marketing firms avoid, so that we are truly showing up as leaders.

Your style in this of course will differ.

But be the honest one.

Be the one not scared to say the thing everyone else is scared to say.

Remember to keep the ending on a positive rather than tearing people down but don't be scared to get real.

Another area not to be overlooked in your strategy is the number of opportunities you give your audience to create user generated content.

For instance, you could quickly stop reading this book, take a snap of yourself with the book, and you could post it on Instagram and tag me @beyond_thedawn.

Oh, you're back! That was quick!

This is a great way for you to generate content you can share without having to do, well much of anything. I want to express that in the digital world there is nothing that shares gratitude the way sharing some content for a creator does. It is really really lovely to receive.

Even better to share!

Give your audience members every opportunity to share with you and for you!

When you give yourself time to build your content, you will need your strategy to help you with the following steps.

The first thing you need to be aware of is what season you are in, in terms of your business but also in consumerism.

Don't neglect thinking about how we are wired into our culture to understand different buying seasons and behaviours throughout the year. Many retailers will hold 60% of their revenue inside the season for Christmas purchasing for instance. When is your industries Christmas time?

You want to make sure your strategy is simple and yet leads your audience through your customer journey in a beautiful way!

Once you have looked at your calendar and determined which areas require your attention, you will be able to build. When you make your strategy, remember you will need to consider any:

- *Statements you feel strongly about sharing*
- *Calendar dates and important seasons*
- *Batch creating for effectiveness*
- *Any Live Launch directives with 6-12 weeks seeding*
- *Review*
- *Repurpose key performing messages.*

All the content you make should be kept somewhere safe like a content bank. I love to use Trello for this! This is so you can reuse it, you can update it and that those assets belong to the company and can be found easily (ideally online) at any moment.

Remember that you are going to be filling different visibilities with your content.

What are the contents I need to fill ?

Your strategy should be a perfect blend of your brand, your messaging and moving your audiences to either stick around for more, or to take the next step in your customer journey.

The worst thing you can do is allow yourself to not show up because you haven't figured out a strategy yet.

However you choose to build it for yourself is fine as long as it works for you - there is no set strategy on how to build one, despite lots of people trying to sell you theirs.

The best one will be the one you build yourself, fully understand, and then can have some input with, when you do seek professional help and outsource in the future.

The strategy of self-expression

Throughout this book I have tripled down on the notion that your content isn't really about you. I stand by it, but I want to explain about the need for you as a creator to share for yourself too. Those of us who are naturals online are those who couldn't hold their water.

We can't help but wear our hearts on our sleeve and we find it really easy to be open about everything.

When we suggest that your content isn't about you, it's because we shouldn't be aiming our content just at self-expression alone. It does need to have more to it than that. It should however have some self-expression. On some level you have a need to be seen, heard, and understood like every other human on the internet.

You should allow yourself the chance to let people see the things about you, that you want them to see.

When we talk mindset, we know that what we think and imagine is what we can achieve.

Sharing the highest version of yourself based on your own comfort can do more for your business and life than merely attracting an audience and it is a worthy journey.

You don't always know who you are inspiring.

Your Values and areas of importance

Your strategy should include areas of communication around your values.

Don't be afraid to frame what you share in a way that highlights what is truly important to you.

Want to have a rant about injustice? Why not? Want to

share an interesting thought - go ahead.

Give your audience plenty of opportunity to connect or disconnect from you.

You may not know what your values are, and there are hundreds of ways to find out, but one of the easiest ways is to think about the last time you were riled up.

Think about something that upset you.

When someone cuts in line in front of you, you may think you are triggered by rude people. You are and you're not.

Something like that, actually highlights a trigger in injustice. The "It's not fair" rule can highlight what is truly important to you in a way you can then share with others.

If you have an instance where you want to share a situation and it will be a learning moment for your audience, then go for it.

The only thing I would suggest is never name and shame.

Remember our ethical rules to use our powers for good, not evil.

Plan vs on the fly

A good plan will allow you some wiggle room to add additional content as you feel it. To jump on trends or discuss todays trending topic. When you preschedule, you take yourself off the hook of having to add the information out on that same day.

You also have a responsibility to review your content, especially if you have or plan to post something that may no longer be appropriate due to a new trend. Ads that mentioned "A new wave" on the day the Thailand Tsunami hit for instance, being pulled by professionals once the news broke.

Some things can't be avoided, but if you have lots of comedy or polarising content, you do need to keep an eye out for situations that may render yesterday's funny joke into a very offensive post, based on trending topics or news out of your control.

Trends

It would be remiss of me to ignore that trends should be part of your strategy to some degree, however the nature of trends is that sometimes you won't know they are coming until they are on your doorstep. You want to look out for them, join in when you can and most importantly have fun.

Entertainment

Entertaining content still is not getting the praise it deserves! I can't tell you how many times pretties have said to me, "I will not dance on TikTok". That's okay! You don't have to, but please do consider the power of your ideal client consuming your content because it is entertaining them. Helping people laugh, learn, or escape for a few moments (more likely seconds) is powerful.

It may not look to immediately be required for your strategy but you will probably find that it is actually really really powerful in terms of audience building and engagement.

Distraction & Being inspired by competition.

One of the worst things you can do is build a strategy that suits your business and then abandon it because of what others are doing. It can be one of the hardest ways for you to get yourself back on track.

Lots of people are testing, trying, and also copying people they are following. If you take that filter back down to your strategy, you are not going to stand out from everyone else in the way you deserve to. No two businesses are the same. Why should your connection strategy be identical to everyone elses?

Stay strong, people do want to hear from you! They don't need to read the same messaging 600 times over from someone else through you.

Whether you believe it or not, there is someone out there who needs to hear it from you. They can't comprehend it from anyone else. Like a soul song, you need to get yourself out there for it to be heard.

CHAPTER TEN -
THE JOURNEY

Insights

You may feel they put the MEH in metric but any data you can see, evaluate and measure in your business is absolutely wonderful in being able to help you to build future strategy.

In professional marketing circles we consider ourselves to be somewhat Data Scientists. We do a lot of experiments and testing and measuring to be able to tell you what works. It is a whole vibe!

Understanding your audience is paramount for any successful business owner. The key to this lies within your insights, data and being able to recognise digital buying behaviours. It's like having a compass in a vast ocean of data, guiding you towards the right decisions.

Insights are your windows into the world of your audience's behaviour, demographics, and interests. Having this information at your fingertips allows you to shape your products or services, your communication, and your delivery methods to better cater to their needs and preferences.

Think about it. Knowing when your audience is most likely to be active and engaged online, you can time your interactions with them strategically, rather than trying to shout over the hustle and bustle of the internet traffic.

Similarly, if you understand which types of content your audience engages with the most, you can focus on creating more of that type, leading to higher engagement rates.

Insights also help you to identify patterns and trends within your audience's behaviour.

If you're attentive, you'll notice any decline in engagement or an unexpected surge of interest in a particular topic. This information is precious, allowing you to tweak your strategy in real time to keep up with your audience's changing preferences.

So, in essence, insights are your trusted companion on the journey of audience building. They help you establish and nurture a strong connection with your audience, ensuring that your strategy is always fine-tuned to their needs and preferences.

Keep an eye on your insights, adjust your strategy accordingly, and watch your business blossom darling!

Repurposing

In a fast-paced digital landscape, where content is king, repurposing has emerged as a game-changing strategy. Gone are the days of creating content in isolation.

Repurposing breathes new life into existing assets, enabling businesses to reach wider audiences, amplify their message, and maximize their return on investment.

By repurposing, we harness the power of versatility. Text becomes videos, blog posts transform into podcasts, and infographics evolve into social media visuals. We adapt, recycle, and innovate, captivating audiences across multiple platforms and catering to diverse preferences.

With careful planning and creativity, repurposing empowers us to optimize resources, reinforce brand consistency, and extend the lifespan of valuable content. It's a strategic approach that not only saves time and effort but also opens doors to fresh opportunities and heightened engagement.

Embrace the art and science of repurposing content, and watch as your message resonates louder, travels farther, and inspires countless minds. The possibilities are endless when we reimagine the potential of what already exists.

Take a look at our repurposing map to see how we often make more out of our outward visibility content!

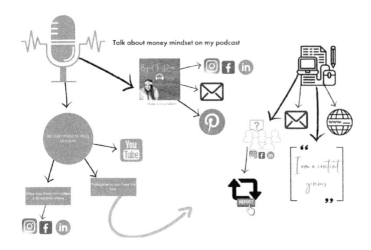

Engagement questions

Engagement is the lifeblood of your social media strategy and it deserves your wholehearted attention.

When you engage with your followers, you're not just having a friendly natter; you're building relationships, boosting your visibility, and showing your audience that they matter to you.

One simple and effective way to spark engagement is by asking questions.

It's like extending an invitation to your audience to share their thoughts and feelings. For example, you might ask, *"What's one thing you've learned this week?"* or *"What's your favourite way to unwind after a busy day?"*

Polls and quizzes are also a delightful way to invite participation. They're fun, interactive, and people just love to share their opinions.

You could pose a question like, *"Which feature do you value most in our product?"* or create a fun quiz, related to your industry.

Finally love, remember to respond to comments and messages promptly and genuinely.

Your followers will appreciate the interaction, feeling heard and valued, and that's a wonderful thing for building strong relationships. So, treat engagement as the heart of your social media strategy, and watch as your business and your relationships flourish.

Monetisation possibilities

A fantastic aspect of building an audience on social media that shouldn't be overlooked. When done right, you can earn additional income direct from your audience building, in your social media accounts. A helpful strategy for normal leads that can have an additional revenue stream for your business.

There are several ways to monetise your audience on social media. Take Instagram, for instance. It offers the feature "Instagram Shopping" that allows businesses to tag their products directly in their posts.

You can earn via gifts/stars and so many other fun sticker exchanges on Facebook, Instagram and TikTok.

Your audience show you love right from inside your posts - videos, how marvellous is that?

YouTube, on the other hand, has the YouTube Partner Program. Once you meet the necessary requirements, such as having a minimum of 1,000 subscribers, you can start earning money from ads displayed on your videos. What's more, YouTube recently introduced "Super Chat," which allows your audience to pay to highlight their messages during your live chats too.

In this arena the possibilities are endless with this side of social media only getting bigger and more experimental.

It's a far cry from when there was only Patreon, a platform where you can provide exclusive content to your audience for a subscription fee. It's an excellent tool for creators to earn a regular income from their most loyal followers.

Remember, Prettie, while monetisation is a wonderful bonus, it's crucial that it doesn't overshadow the primary reason for your social media presence: to build relationships and engage with your audience.

Keep a balanced approach, and your business will grow not just in revenue, but in audience loyalty too.

Funnels

A term you may have heard buzzing around: the marketing funnel is definitely something you want to consider as part of your online social behaviours. In the simplest terms, it's a model that illustrates the journey customers take from the moment they become aware of your business and brand. It brings them through a customer journey to understand your products or service until they make a purchase.

A sales funnel is usually divided into stages: awareness, consideration, and decision. It is entirely different to an audience building funnel, and you do need to know which one you are wanting, before you go ahead and build, or hire an agency like ours to build one for you.

In terms of social media, you can use this funnel to guide your audience towards your email list. You can start by creating awareness with engaging posts that attract your audience's attention.

Then, you can foster consideration by offering valuable content and demonstrating your expertise in your field.

You can encourage your audience to sign up to your email list, often in exchange for something of value such as an exclusive piece of content, often referred to as a "freebie", a discount code, or early access to a new product or service.

Why is this important for your social media strategy? Well, an email list is like your golden ticket.

It's a direct line of communication to your audience, free from the ever-changing algorithms of social media platforms and cannot be taken away by those same platforms with a glitch or deactivation of your account.

By growing your email list, you're not just increasing your chances of converting followers into customers, but also building a community that values what you offer, opening up communication in a beautiful way.

And that, darling, is something worth taking very seriously.

For the top of the funnel, you'll want to create content that piques interest and attracts new followers. This could be anything from engaging posts, attention-grabbing visuals, educational videos, to intriguing questions.

The goal here is to get your brand noticed and start a conversation.

Next, we move to the "consideration" stage. Here, your focus should be on deepening the relationship with your audience.

Provide valuable, engaging content that positions your business as a trusted source. Share customer testimonials, showcase your products or services in action, offer tips and advice, or highlight the unique aspects of your brand. The aim is to keep your audience engaged and coming back for more.

Finally, in the "decision" stage, you want to drive your audience towards action. This is where you encourage them to sign up for your email list. A common tactic is to offer an incentive, such as exclusive content, a special discount, or early access to products or services. These "lead magnets" can be promoted through social media posts, ads, or direct messages.

When your audience signs up for your email list, they're expressing a deeper interest in your brand. This provides an excellent opportunity to nurture these relationships further, through personalised email marketing, fostering loyalty, and ultimately guiding your audience towards making a purchase.

Marketing Budget

Yes prettie, you do need one!

When it comes to running a successful business, setting

a budget for digital marketing is as important as having a fabulous product or service. It provides a financial blueprint that guides your marketing efforts, ensuring you allocate your resources effectively to maximise your return on investment.

Not having a digital marketing budget is like trying to navigate a ship without a compass - you might keep moving, but you'll find it difficult to reach your destination.

One common pitfall new businesses and solo entrepreneurs often face is overlooking the importance of a digital marketing budget. Some might see it as an unnecessary expense rather than an investment. This approach, darling, can lead to missed opportunities for growth and can also have a detrimental effect on business success.

With a carefully planned budget, you can invest in areas that bring the most value to your business. Perhaps it's improving your website's SEO, investing in social media advertising, creating high-quality content, or employing email marketing strategies. A budget will help you prioritise, track your expenditure, measure your results, and make strategic adjustments as necessary.

Also, a budget allows you to test and experiment with different marketing strategies. Without one, you may hesitate to try new things due to fear of overspending. But with a budget in place, you can allocate funds for experimentation, discover what works best for your business, and adjust your strategies accordingly.

In conclusion darling, setting a digital marketing budget

is not just a task to check off your to-do list. It's an integral part of your business strategy that can pave the way for growth and success. So take the time to create a budget that reflects your goals, aligns with your resources, and maximises your potential.

A simple marketing budget can be created using a spreadsheet, and it should provide a clear view of your planned marketing activities, their costs, and the results they deliver.

Here's a simple example of what a digital marketing budget template could look like:

Marketing Category: This column lists the different marketing channels you plan to use. For example, social media advertising, content creation, email marketing, SEO services, and so on.

Description: This column provides additional details about each activity. For example, under social media advertising, you might note, "Facebook Ads campaign for product launch."

Projected Cost: Here, you list the expected cost for each activity. This can include costs for software, ad spend, agency fees, and so forth.

Actual Cost: This is where you record what you actually spend on each activity. Tracking this helps you stay within your budget and provides useful data for future budget planning.

Projected ROI (Return on Investment): This column is for your estimated return based on your spending. For example, if you're spending £100 on social media advertising, how much revenue do you expect to generate from that expenditure?

Actual ROI: Similar to the actual cost, the actual ROI column is where you record the real return you received from each marketing activity.

Remember darling, that a marketing budget isn't set in stone. It's a living document that you should revisit and adjust regularly based on your business's performance and the changing marketing landscape. Consider it your financial guide to making smart and strategic marketing decisions!

AI

AI, or artificial intelligence, has started to create a buzz. It's shaping up to be a powerful tool in the world of digital marketing, opening up possibilities we could hardly dream of a few years ago. AI can process vast amounts of data in the blink of an eye, generate suggestions based on patterns, and even produce content. It's all rather remarkable!

However, even with all its capabilities, AI should never be the sole author of a brand's content. AI is smart, but it lacks the one thing that truly sets humans apart - our ability to feel and express complex emotions.

It's this emotional connection that forms the heart and soul of great content. It's our shared experiences, our shared joys and struggles, that resonate with audiences and create that strong bond between a brand and its customers.

When everyone is using AI for content (which is

already beginning to happen) the real human artform of copywriting will become more valuable still. Standing out in a way that AI cannot. This is a skill not to be lost because there are new tools to support it.

AI simply cannot match the depth and richness of human emotion. It's not capable of experiencing the world as we do, with all its highs and lows, its triumphs and challenges. And while AI is rapidly evolving, it will always lack the capability to authentically express, understand, and connect on a deep emotional level. AI has no bad ex's, no funny stories of its own, no trauma, no loss, no love, no joy.

AI has never felt the breeze in its hair, the tingles of music down its arms or been able to smell summer rain.

That's not to say AI doesn't have a place in content creation. It can certainly help with tasks like data analysis, keyword research, and even content drafting. But the final touch, the emotional connection, should always be a human endeavour.

And while it is an incredible tool that's changing the digital marketing landscape, it's just that - a tool. It should complement our efforts, not replace them. The power of human emotion in content creation is something that simply cannot be replicated by artificial intelligence, and we should cherish and harness it.

After all, it's what makes us wonderfully, tragically and innately connected as humans.

THANK YOU

When I share the information I do, I think of you. I think of you being able to attend your children's sports day.

Delighting in another paid invoice making this month so much easier for you.

I love to imagine you earning enough to buy that holiday, take the time off.

To care for your parents.

To care for yourself!

I think about you not worrying about bills or being able to open that second business or even buying multiple properties.

I think about you walking into Chanel and picking out the thing you want without even caring what the price tag says.

I think about you walking through Tesco not counting as

you throw items in your cart.

I also think of how we will laugh together when you get your first scary tax bill that is more than you used to earn in a year!

We start businesses to enhance our lives and in doing so we affect others, often so positively that the ripple effect goes **beyond** that which we can easily measure.

Join us in my free group to discuss these and many more ideas in terms of you being able to create your own version of a successful business via the medium of audience building, (notice how we didn't call the book - how to get more leads, although we may have sold more if we had)

Our free forever group: https://www.facebook.com/groups/ Socialmediacommunitygroup/

And once you have read it, if you haven't folded all the pages, or scribbled in the margins or highlighted important "aha" moments, then please pass it on to another business owner or entrepreneur.

Share the wealth of knowledge and interesting ideas with others.

Offer it as a reading group feature or give to a charity shop!

Pass the ripple effect on as far as you can reach, because I may have started this particular connection thread, but it is you that will determine its breadth and reach, in continuing the chain to others who needed it just as much as we have.

In passing this little piece of love on to another, you may

spark something wonderful for us all.

ABOUT THE AUTHOR

Dawn Baxter, the esteemed owner of Beyond the Dawn Digital Limited, is a true industry leader, expert, and mentor in the realm of digital marketing. With her unwavering passion for social media marketing, organic content strategies, and positive psychology, Dawn has cemented her position as a sought-after authority in the field.

With an illustrious career in sales, luxury branding and digital marketing, spanning over a decade, Dawn has honed her skills and expertise to perfection. Her deep understanding of social media platforms and their dynamics enables her to devise innovative strategies that drive exceptional results for her clients.

Dawn's keen eye for trends and her ability to craft engaging content has propelled numerous brands to new heights of success.

What truly sets Dawn apart is her commitment to using positive psychology principles in her work. She understands that creating meaningful connections with audiences goes beyond mere promotion—it's about building authentic relationships.

By leveraging her expertise in positive psychology, Dawn empowers brands to connect with their target audience on a deeper level, fostering genuine loyalty and brand advocacy.

Beyond her remarkable achievements, Dawn is also recognised as a mentor and guide to aspiring marketers. She selflessly shares her knowledge and experiences, helping others navigate the complex world of digital marketing.

Dawn's friendly yet authoritative demeanour makes her approachable, and her mentorship has inspired many professionals to excel in their careers.

In 2023 Dawns Audience Attraction Certification course for social media managers, was awarded the only UK quality standard trademark for social media management and strategy in the UK, making her methods the benchmark of exceptional quality in this previously unregulated field.

Dawn Baxter is an industry luminary whose expertise in social media marketing, organic content strategies, and positive psychology has solidified her reputation as an exceptional leader, expert, and mentor.

Her unwavering dedication to her craft, combined with

her personable nature, make her a true asset to the digital marketing community.

P.s. She didn't write this about herself, but she did squeal with delight when reading it!

CITED SOURCES

1. Bronte sisters
2. Star Trek
3. Kill Bill - film
4. Erik Erikson (1963). Childhood and society. W. W. Norton & Company.
5. ABBA
6. Rosenberg, M. (1965). Society and the adolescent self-image. Princeton university press.
7. Côté, J. E., & Schwartz, S. J. (2002). Comparing psychological and sociological approaches to identity: Identity status, identity capital, and the individualization process. Journal of Adolescence, 25(6), 571-586.
8. Michelle Pfeffier
9. Rachel Green - F.R.I.E.N.D.S
10. Jacqui Leonard
11. Dunning Kruger - imposter syndrome theory
12. Breadface
13. Bell Delphine

14. Mr Mackey - Southpark
15. Donald Trump
16. Roe VS Wade
17. Erin Brockovich
18. Nary Poppins
19. Freddie Mercury
20. Tim Curry
21. Lee Strasberg
22. Konstantin Stanislavski
23. Henri Tajfel.